Practical Bamboos

Practical Bamboos

The 50 Best Plants for Screens, Containers and More

Paul Whittaker

Timber Press

Portland | London

Dedication

I dedicate this book to one very important individual, my wife Diana, without whom it would never have been finished. In the hardest, coldest and most worrying of winters of my life in business, you have smiled cheerfully when I've been grumpy or down, offered unending support and, quite rightly, suggestions and criticism. You have checked, proofed, altered and directed me, all without any worry. Most of all, you have been there – always in, or close to, my presence.

You have all my love. X

← Frontispiece: The glistening foliage and well spaced culms of *Phyllostachys vivax* (left) offer light shade and a strong visual contrast alongside a hosta

Published in 2010 by Timber Press, Inc.

The Haseltine Building
133 s.w. Second Avenue, Suite 450
Portland, Oregon 97204-3527

2 The Quadrant
135 Salusbury Road
London NW6 6RJ

www.timberpress.com

www.timberpress.co.uk

ISBN-13: 978-1-60469-056-9

Designed by Dick Malt

Printed in China

Catalogue records for this book are also available from the Library of Congress and the British Library.

Contents

↑ *Phyllostachys* culms
reaching for the sky

Preface

As the owner of a bamboo nursery, visitors to my premises frequently ask me which bamboo is my favourite. After twenty years of growing them, this is never the easiest question to answer. Many of the enquirers are beginners on a quest to acquire their first bamboo, while others are addicts who don't want to miss out on an essential addition to their collection. Old and new customers alike use this question as an opening gambit to seek out good advice, something that you should never make a bamboo purchase without and also hopefully one of the reasons you are reading this book.

Out of some 350 or more temperate bamboos, approximately one quarter of these are available for general sale and around half are available in very small quantities annually, invariably from specialist nurseries. The remaining quarter are extremely rare due to difficulty in propagation, finicky growing methods or hoarding by addicted amateurs – to acquire one of these, you will undoubtedly need to go on a waiting list or get involved in some serious bribing and bartering. For the purposes of this book, a number of the generally available bamboos will make up the majority of the selection featured here, with a few rare examples thrown in to whet your appetite for more of a challenge in years to come. All of the bamboos included in this book have been tried and tested. As a group, they are versatile and valuable garden plants that cover a wide range of heights, habits and uses. There are no disappointments here and I often tell my customers that if they don't succeed with these, they should give up on bamboos completely!

To return to the opening question, I don't really have a favourite bamboo, although I did write in my previous book, *Hardy Bamboos: Taming the Dragon*, that *Phyllostachys aureosulcata* f. *spectabilis* would be my desert island bamboo, meaning that if I could choose only one, this would be it. To repeat a famous British television slogan, "It does everything it says on the tin", meaning that this plant has all the characteristics that a good bamboo should: colourful culms (canes), evergreen leaves and is very hardy and quick to mature so is good value for money. A few years on, I now find it much more difficult to name any one particular bamboo as my favourite. There are many bamboos of hugely varying habit, character and quality that I would not be able to garden successfully without. All of my favourites are easy to recommend because I know the likely success that a beginner will have with them, particularly when given the right information and advice to go with them. But be aware, success with bamboos can often become an obsession, especially when you experience the individual beauty of bamboos, their ease of cultivation and the speedy transformation of a young plant into maturity. I know about the perils of addiction because it happened to me. After all, supplying a potential failure to someone with no previous experience with bamboos would be a tactless mistake – I've often been known to withhold or hide the rare and the difficult, even though very beautiful, from those new to bamboo, so failure is never an option.

However, the plants aside, the main object of this book is to portray and present a range of bamboos worthy of almost any garden situation. This reminds me of the second question I am most frequently asked, "Can you recommend a bamboo for … ?" This question is invariably followed by one or more of a huge range of requests, such as screening from neighbours or eyesores, windbreaks, groves for the children to play in, pots on patios and roof gardens,

↑ The lush greenery of bamboos providing shade in the summer

pond-side features, preventing erosion on slopes or just for general use. These are just some of the different qualities my customers look for (and find) in bamboos.

During the last five decades, the way we now think, live and garden has dramatically changed. Gardening practices have generally become more adventurous, artistic and even flamboyant in style. Bamboos will undoubtedly continue to play an important part in the ever-changing approaches to modern gardening, but I would, however, urge you not to become too entrenched in "flavour of the month" gardening styles or fashions. Don't overly subscribe to the occasionally brash and/or mordant remarks of the media, which can utterly condemn a style or a particular plant group with a few words or a brief rant from a garden presenter. These are usually individual preferences and do not stem from truths.

You should start with an understanding of your own preferences, needs and styles, a few ideas to build upon and a little guidance. I am writing this book to help you choose wisely and limit your mistakes, but most of all to enlighten you to the endless possibilities for using bamboos in your garden.

Introduction

← Not quite a jungle, but the climate of southern France can produce some astonishing results

One of bamboo's remarkable qualities is the fact that it is able to propagate in a diverse range of global natural habitats. The wide variety of habits, types and forms of bamboo render it useful not just in gardening and landscaping, but also as a sustainable and long-lived woody material. Bamboos' adaptability and usefulness in many sites and planting aspects has now been noticed and their popularity has increased as a response to this upsurge in interest.

↑ A selection of bamboo culms showing variation in shape and form

Choices – Know What Your Options Are

For many people, their first thought or vision of a bamboo is of a tropical giant from a wild equatorial jungle, with a lofty culm (cane) structure towering skywards. For others, it's the lush verdancy of subtropical foliage dripping in the rain, or silhouetted against an exotic sunset.

Although not tropical, the bamboos portrayed in this book can provide the same imagery for you in your garden. The bamboos featured here are hardy temperate plants that are nearly all evergreen and are also, without a doubt, some of the strongest plants used in gardening, as many of these bamboos are native to much harsher climes than our own. Their winter greenery and almost constant movement will add a very different dimension to any garden.

Choices can be made as to bamboos' foliage and culms, specimen planting or ground cover, compactness, screening abilities, meandering groves or greenery. Habits vary from the reliably tight clump formers to the incredibly invasive, with plenty in between. Heights range between 30 cm (1 ft.) to 14 m (46 ft.) or more in very favourable locations. Culm colours are usually striking, ranging from gold through to blue and green and on to tinted red, deep purple and black. Culms sometimes also include mottles, blotches, streaks, striping and occasional swellings, distortions and zigzag shaping. Foliage is equally varied, ranging from thin, almost needle-like leaves to massive platter-sized ones, usually in tones of green. However, across the different genera some plants have striking leaf and culm variegations ranging from white, cream and yellow stripes to streaks and/or mottling. Combine some of these variations across the different plants and you have a recipe for a group of outstanding ornamental plants.

Bad Press – Putting the Rumours to Rest

Before we delve into a few interesting and even curious facts about bamboos, the record has to be set straight about the "dissing down" that these plants sometimes suffer. There have been many discreditable and disparaging myths circulating about bamboos recently, but throughout this book many of these will be put to rest.

Gardeners who view bamboos with trepidation can rest assured that not all of them are invasive. In fact, many of them are tightly clump forming, with the new shoots never deviating more than a few fingers away from the mother clump annually. In addition to this, not all bamboos die after flowering – all are evergreen barring a meagre few. If a bamboo is not showing all its foliar glory, there is usually a problem that is easily explained and remedied. Bamboos are also no more expensive than many other plant groups that are produced in good variety almost entirely by specialists, but bamboos will at least provide lots of pleasure and quick results from your investment. Temperate bamboos are extremely hardy, with many tolerating a minimum of −20°C (−4°F) in zone 6, with a good handful able to take the extremes of −29°C (−20°F) in zone 4, although these are likely to suffer some (fixable) winter damage.

Last but not least, bamboos are certainly not difficult to grow, being suited to a wide range of extremes and growing conditions. This results in an abundance of possible uses in most gardens and landscapes, as they require the minimum of fuss, preferring to grow at their own pace while building up their own food reserves and generally adapting to their surrounds naturally.

A few imposters – finding the fakes

There are a few plants that are commonly mistaken for bamboo. A few are good ornamentals and one or two obnoxious to the extreme, mainly on account of their colonizing abilities.

Japanese knotweed (*Fallopia japonica, Polygonum cuspidatum*)

This plant has hollow, jointed stems that are similar in structure to bamboo, but this plant is herbaceous and spreads voraciously via underground rhizomes, which is possibly a contributing factor to the negative views some hold about bamboo. Japanese knotweed has large, heart-shaped leaves and white flower spikes, while most bamboo leaves are tiny in comparison. It is notoriously difficult to eradicate as it can propagate itself from the tiniest piece of rhizome left in soil. Once established, it mulches the soil and can smother all other herbaceous plants and grass in its vicinity. It is often seen on the boundaries and in the woodlands of large estates and also commonly on railway embankments. This is one of the most pernicious plants ever to be introduced into a landscape.

Giant reed (*Arundo donax*)

This plant (pictured overleaf) has a similar, cane-like structure to bamboo, but the leaves are blue-green,

long and tapered and are directly attached to the stems, whereas bamboo leaves are attached to the culms' branches.

In cool temperate gardens, this is valued as a good ornamental feature plant, as it rises up well beyond head height and has a bold, architectural quality to it. In warmer areas similar to the Mediterranean climate where it originates, it can become a nuisance as it relishes warmth and moisture.

→ A walkway with an arch created from dried bamboo culms (canes)

Horsetail (*Equisetum hyemale*)

The horizontal banding on the hollow, rush-like stems is similar in structure to bamboo culms, although this plant (pictured left) and all its other forms is perennial in habit. Often sold as an aquatic or water garden plant, it does have an ethereal appearance in the right place. It also has a propensity to run amok with its very slender root structure, which is difficult to eradicate and it has earned a reputation as a pest in warmer regions.

Heavenly bamboo (*Nandina domestica*)

Actually a woody shrub from the Barberry (*Berberis*) family, this plant bears no physical resemblance to bamboo at all, except for its vertical structure and fans of leaves at the top of the stalks. It has white flowers and red berries and is really only confused with bamboo because of its misleading common name.

Amur silver grass (*Miscanthus sacchariflorus*)

Often called Sugar Cane *Miscanthus* as it bears some resemblance to the aforementioned food plant of the tropics. Very tall and vigorous, growing up to 4 m (13 ft.), with long and arching strap-like leaves attached to quite woody stems, although technically a perennial. Now cultivated as a bio-mass fuel on account of its speed of growth and regenerative qualities. Its silvery flower heads are very attractive, but it is shy to flower in cool gardens. This plant is mistaken for bamboo because of its imposing size and subtropical impact.

Bamboo palm (*Chamaedorea seifrizii*)

The common name and the white scars on the trunk of this palm are the main reasons why it is sometimes mistaken for bamboo. It is a very slow growing, beautiful indoor palm that erupts fresh greenery from the top of its trunk.

Lucky bamboo (*Dracaena sanderiana*)

Last but not least, the bane of all bamboo growers – this is not a bamboo and should never have been given the misleading common name. This plant roots quickly and propagates in water, which is also how it is frequently packaged and sold. The nodes on the green stems are the only resemblance it shares with bamboo. It is not hardy and is available for purchase from all and sundry, except bamboo nurseries, so request it at your peril!

Fascinating Facts – Things to Know About Bamboo

Well over a thousand uses for bamboo have been recorded over the years, but one could easily come up with many more using a little imagination and innovation. While many of these uses won't apply within most gardens, they are nevertheless interesting, so just a few are mentioned here amongst some other points of interest:

Bamboo has been and will continue to be used widely as a material in everyday life. Indeed, all of the following products may be made from bamboo or from one of its elements – houses, scaffolding, boats and eating utensils. Some parts of bamboos are also edible and some parts of specific species are used in traditional Chinese and southern Asian Ayurvedic medicine and acupuncture. Bamboos are also frequently used in the practices and symbolism of many Eastern religions and have been known to contribute to the culture and arts of many east Asian countries. However, in the planet's current state of ecological disarray, it is important to note that bamboos can play a valuable role in helping to secure a better balance between humanity and the planet we inhabit. Tropical bamboos, admittedly, are able to play a more important role than the ornamental temperate bamboos described in this book, mainly because of their impressive regenerative ability and the vast areas they cover, particularly in countries where there is an element of rural poverty and underdevelopment. Nevertheless, here are a few facts that will explain and qualify the wonderment of bamboo.

Bamboo can be sustainably harvested and is also annually renewable as it produces new culms, unlike timber, where the whole plant is destroyed when harvested and takes many years to replace. As well as this cycle of impressive regeneration, bamboo produces more oxygen and consumes more carbon dioxide pro rata than any other plant in the world. Bamboo is the fastest growing plant on earth and even in my garden there have been 12 m (40 ft.) culms produced in summer during a six-week period. In the tropics, mature plants are capable of growth in excess of 1 m (3.3 ft.) a day. Bamboos' resilience also enabled them to be the first plant to regain a foothold in the scorched and sterile earth in Hiroshima and Nagasaki, Japan after the atomic bombings in World War II. Bamboos also have a unique ability to make toxic substances inert in soils, as well as being tolerant of air pollution. Apart from being food for the giant panda, bamboo branches and leaves also provide fodder for many other animals and when dried and can also be used as litter or bedding.

Woody canes that are dried from bamboo culms have a higher tensile strength than steel and are frequently used for scaffolding and reinforcement in eastern Asia. As well as this tensile strength, bamboo canes have great flexibility and have proved to be resistant to earthquakes. Bamboo provides not just shelter but also food and is a crucial part of many economies. The production of bamboo shoots is also a sizeable and viable industry, as Taiwan alone is responsible for the consumption of eighty thousand tons annually.

Bamboo is now being touted as a fashionable flooring option in the West, while bamboo clothing is becoming favoured with its eco-friendly characteristics. Manufacturers of clothing made from bamboo can boast some interesting facts and statistics – bamboo fibres are absorbent yet don't stick to the skin, are strong, durable and warm in cool weather and cool in hot weather due to their breathable quality. They are antibacterial, anti-static, uv-protective and do not irritate allergy-prone skin, as well as being totally biodegradable. On an environmental note, bamboo also uses much less water than cotton, thrives perfectly without pesticides or fertilizers, doesn't destroy the land as with cotton production and can grow on steep slopes where many other crops are not able to. The yield of any given area of bamboo is ten times more than that of cotton. Countries such as India, Burma and China have also noted that there is a much faster return on investment from bamboo than on other plantations and there are now over twenty million hectares of bamboo plantations in Asia.

The interwoven structure of a bamboo rhizome system is ideal for soil conservation, due to its anti-erosion properties, which is why bamboo is already used in many areas of Japan for reinforcing fragile riversides. Bamboo can also be planted in deforested areas and where mudslides occur, as the canopy of bamboo leaves and branches disperses and reduces the power of monsoon rainfall in volatile environments. Bamboo thus has many valuable qualities – aside from the above economic and global uses, on a smaller scale it also offers shade and sanctuary, shelter for roosting birds, protection against wind and noise and most of all, speedy development and evergreen beauty.

What and Where – How It All Started

In the grand scheme of planetary evolution, bamboos can be traced back to their origins some thirty million years ago. The now many different forms have evolved from ancient broadleaved tropical grasses and are very similar in structure and growing habits to the modern day grass family. The exceptions to this are that most bamboos are now very woody instead of having herbaceous qualities and that temperate bamboos do not flower annually. In summary, bamboos can clearly be described as tall or shrubby grass with woody stems (culms).

Their Place on Earth

Including the tropical forms, bamboos cover large tracts both north and south of the equator and occur naturally in most areas of the world, excepting Europe and the North and South Poles.

In broad terms, temperate bamboos have evolved from either the plants from the ancient plains and lowlands of eastern China, Taiwan, the Korean peninsula, Japan and the neighbouring northern Kuril and Sakhalin islands. Most bamboos don't need to flower to increase their fold. Instead they mostly propagate by their spread of underground rhizomes, forming new plants or colonies; *Phyllostachys* is one such example. The remaining temperate bamboos have evolved from plants in the foothills, lower mountains and valleys of the relatively more recently developed mountain ranges such as the Andes and the Himalayas. The bamboos found here are newly developed, with temperate bamboos from this group being almost always tight clump forming. These montane bamboos generally need to flower once in their life cycle to reproduce.

A few notes about flowering

Bamboo flowers are not a permanent or even regular visual part of the plant and they do not affect bamboos' growing habits or structure. In fact, bamboos' flowering relates more to the habitat of the plant and how the plant's style and/or need for reproduction have evolved. Although little is known about the flowering cycle of bamboo, this subject is one of the most questioned about bamboos and therefore deserves a lengthy explanation.

There has been much thought as to why bamboos flower and towards their irregular and unpredictable flowering cycle in particular. The intervals of time between flowerings is variable to say the least – it ranges from ten to two hundred or more years, depending on the source of information. However, it must be noted that there are more species that have never flowered, as opposed to the few that have, since scientific plant records began some two hundred years ago. In comparison to many other plants in our landscapes, except perhaps large trees, bamboos are very long-lived.

On some species and forms, flowering occurs regularly and the plants are never affected. On others, when flowering occurs the bamboo is often temporarily checked in its development. For example, new culms and/or leaves may not prosper during flowering because the plant's resources will be diverted to the flowers, however, many bamboos do recover from these temporary set backs. Some can also produce small amounts of seed during the flowering process, which is a particular bonus for members of the nursery trade who wish to increase stock. The seeds are usually solid and the size of a cereal grain, not to be confused with the fleshy husk that surrounds it. Seeds are usually produced in summer after a late winter or early spring flowering,

as bamboo flowers are wind pollinated. Seeds must be collected as soon as they are ripe or ready to drop (before the birds do it for you) and sown on the surface of some potting mix and covered with a sprinkling of sharp sand. If seeds are initially stored and sown later, they sometimes become dormant and difficult to germinate. It has been noted that some bamboos flower only on a few branches or on just one or two culms in a grove during a single year. This almost always has no detrimental effect on the plant.

The worst-case scenario is complete or gregarious flowering where every culm and branch of the bamboo flowers, leaf production is halted and no new food can be produced. Combined with this, existing food reserves in the rhizome are used in the flowering cycle and so the whole plant will weaken and may die. Should you be unfortunate enough to witness this, the only saving grace is that at least seed is more likely to be produced. It has even been known for the occasional specimen to recover

↑ Seedlings of *Fargesia nitida* from just a few weeks after germination (left), to three years old (right)

after appearing to be dead – this is most likely due to the effective food storage of a very mature rhizome system where all the reserves have not been diminished by flowering, but such rejuvenation in younger plants would be less likely. There is also the remarkable fact that if flowering occurs on one genetic species, it will flower worldwide irrespective of the age or location of the bamboo.

There are no generalizations here as there is little confirmed knowledge on the specifics of bamboo flowering, but as a general rule clumping bamboos' inability to spread makes them more likely to succumb to a flowering cycle rather than those that can spread. The only unanswered question is "When?"

Climate and Habitat

The areas of the world that temperate bamboos inhabit and the individual climatic conditions they tolerate have much bearing on how and where bamboos best perform in our gardens. When it comes to the plants, a minimum hardiness has been attributed to each one, this being the minimum temperature it will tolerate before death is likely to occur. Up to this extreme temperature, the bamboo may not look too good in various ways, including possible leaf loss, some culm and branch death and rhizome damage due to frost penetrating the ground. Bamboos do however have an unbelievable ability to recover from almost total annihilation due to harsh conditions because of the food storage capacity of the rhizomes. Some of the clumping forms may take longer to recover than those with more spreading habits, on account of their compact rhizome system, which stores less under the ground for them to recover with. All of this may sound disconcerting, but the climate zones exist to prompt you to grow plants suitable for your zone and not those on the borderlines which would suffer from extreme temperatures.

The main concern for gardeners is the suitability of a plant for their garden and its ability to perform and survive. Much has been written on the internet regarding the experiences of other gardeners (especially in gardening blogs), with many giving information and recommending guidelines for other gardeners. Stories of success, failure and reasons for either are also often shared. When it comes to discovering what will grow in your area, finding someone in your locality with previous experience is the best guide you can have. The hardiness zones are actually very limiting as they only take temperatures into account while heat, wind, high humidity, salt exposure, drought or arid conditions can all have

an effect on certain types of bamboo. It is very difficult to generalize but there are bamboos that will not adapt well to inland or continental climates, usually areas with long, hot and arid summers or in other cases areas with a high heat and degree of humidity. Many of the clumping forms described throughout this book prefer cooler, more temperate and usually maritime climates. *Fargesia*, *Borinda* and *Thamnocalamus* originate from a mountainous area, and as such prefer cooler and moister conditions. When planted in arid conditions, the leaves tend

↑ This *Fargesia robusta* flattened by heavy snowfall will spring back upwards when its covering melts

to roll up like needles, a sign of stress and lack of natural water protection from excessive transpiration. *Chusquea* species however are slightly more adaptable, originating from a wider variety of habitats, some cool to almost snowline in elevation, while others will propagate in warm and humid forests and as such can adapt to a wider range of climate zones.

↑ *Fargesia* and other clump formers
prefer a cooler temperate climate

↑ These lush bamboos are proving their
evergreen qualities in the depths of winter

Phyllostachys species have been mentioned as runners, especially in their native habitat of China where they form small forests, but also in warm, almost Mediterranean climates. However in cool areas, many species are much less aggressive to the point of being frustrating (according to a few growers who would probably like more stock to propagate from). Although equally beautiful regardless of stature, the growth habits of bamboos in cooler areas can be much more compact with enhanced colouring. For example, a timber bamboo in zone 6 may remain compact and juvenile like a montane bamboo for many years and never have the very thick culm structure and height it should (although some will surprise and even after a decade or two in the ground may suddenly mature with monstrous culms appearing unexpectedly). In zone 8, the same bamboo is likely to be more open in habit and mature

more quickly, producing taller and thicker culms purely on account of the more favourable climate. The easiest way to explain this is to impress on you the fact that you can never have tall, giant or thick culm structure without an equally substantial rhizome structure below the ground to give support and anchorage for the culms.

Young plants are also always more susceptible to winter damage than a bamboo that has been established for a few years in its place in the garden, as larger clumps are always more resilient. It is always worth protecting a young plant with netting or a windbreak before the onset of potential bad weather, particularly if you are trying a bamboo that is on the borderline of your hardiness zone. Microclimates of sheltered town and city gardens that are blessed with the ever present radiant heat emissions from buildings, concrete and tarmac allow the gardener to be more adventurous, as even a degree or two in increased annual average temperature can be enough to grow a bamboo that might otherwise be impossible. In summary, without trying you will never know, but rather than suffer disappointment or expensive losses, seek out other gardeners who have possibly tried your intended bamboo before you.

Soils

Bamboos are really no different in their needs to the vast majority of garden plants and are adaptable to most types of soil except the very dry and desert-like or the extremely wet. However, dry and impoverished soils can be improved by the addition of organic matter to increase their moisture holding capacity. One or two species, as will be mentioned in the plant selections, are more tolerant of wet conditions than others, however young plants will not establish when the conditions are too wet. Mature plants will tolerate reasonable periods of wetness at the base, but generally bamboos need to breathe as well as drink at the roots. To allow young plants to reach proportions

where they can tolerate wetter conditions, I would suggest planting on shallow mounds of imported soil, above the wet layer below, thus allowing the young plant to breathe. Clay soils are rarely a problem due to the penetrating strength of a bamboo rhizome, but do make sure the plant has a good start with a well-worked and friable soil to start with.

Bamboos are tolerant of a wide range in pH (acidity and alkalinity). Although said to prefer the slightly acid, they will do well on alkaline soils, but sometimes will be paler in leaf in the latter soil. My own garden is slightly alkaline, in some areas consisting of shallow chalky boulder-clay, but all the bamboos perform brilliantly. The ones on the clay admittedly had a slower start in life, but they are no less healthy for it. In one of my customers' gardens, the soil is so acid in parts that only moss will grow. However, in slightly less acid parts where there has been no previous excavation or dredging, he manages to succesfully grow representatives from most of the genera.

The best indicator of whether a soil is suitable is that where few other plants grow successfully, neither will bamboos.

Bamboo Structure and Growing Habits

Without stating the obvious, the main structural parts of a bamboo are the underground root and rhizome system and the above ground culms that also support the branches and foliage. However, there is a little more to it than this, because the bamboo plant is quite unique in its formation and all its different parts have an important role to play. Although bamboos are members of the grass family, they are notably different from this family's other members on account of their usually woody and dominant structure. When compared to trees and/or shrubs, it

becomes clear that bamboos have no obvious central growth point, such as a stem or trunk, that expands in girth and height. Instead a colony of individual stems is continually formed on an annual cycle below ground.

Both the rhizomes that support the bamboo and the culms that arise from them are divided into segments with alternating solid nodes or joints and usually hollow internodes or sections. The hollowness of the culms is one reason for their flexibility in all weathers. The growth points are the solid nodes

↑ The strong timber-like culms of
Phyllostachys vivax

↑ The two main types of rhizome systems,
clumping (top) and running (bottom)

where the roots, buds or culms emerge from the rhizomes, or the branches that carry the leaves emerge from the culms. The only non-segmented parts of a bamboo are found on its extremities, including the feeding roots and the leaves that make use of the sunlight. The food and water that is taken in from the soil and converted into usable plant food through photosynthesis is then stored in the plant's rhizomes. This enables the bamboo to reproduce new underground parts to generate and support new culms above.

Below Ground

Purchase a young bamboo from a nursery and they will normally tell you what increase in growth the plant is capable of within a few years, usually without you having to ask. One of the key points that should be mentioned, especially to a beginner, is that "You

can't have shoots without roots," or, said another way, "Root before shoot." This emphasizes that the most important parts of the bamboo plant, its roots and rhizome, are responsible for the individual plant's structure and development.

The rhizomes are the main underground structure of the bamboo, as they produce and support the eventually weighty top growth and store the bamboo's food reserves. Different types of rhizome systems will produce plants of a completely different appearance and structure. There are basically two main types of rhizome structures and put simply, they are clumping (pachymorph) and running (leptomorph), with a few slight variations within and between the two. It is worth noting at this point that a clumping bamboo can never be aggressive, although they can grow quite large in terms of final height and girth. However, a running bamboo can appear as a tight clump for many years and then suddenly go wandering afar, although there are many variables that affect this, such as climate and soil conditions. In cold gardens, some aggressors will remain tight in habit, behaving like clumping bamboos for virtually all their lives because the shorter growing season and cooler soil impedes the full development of their rhizome systems.

→ A clumping *Fargesia*

Clump formers

This rhizome type mainly supports groups of tropical and subtropical bamboos such as the genus *Bambusa*. Unfortunately, tropical and subtropical bamboos are not covered here as this book's focus is on hardy forms that are suitable for use in temperate gardens. However, there are a unique group of montane bamboos that do have a clumping habit, such as *Borinda*, *Chusquea*, *Fargesia* and *Thamnocalamus* and many species within these genera. Many of these bamboos are thus most useful in temperate gardens. Clumping rhizomes are usually thick and bulbous, with very short sections or necks that are joined together. This short neck gives the bamboo its clumping habit, as if the rhizomes are close together, the culms will also grow closely to each other above ground. The tips of the rhizomes curve upwards and narrow towards a point that will form a new culm during the next growing season. The feeding roots are always much finer than the rhizomes themselves, while new rhizomes emerge from the congested nodes, or growth points, on the swollen part of the rhizome. The rhizomes of clumping bamboos are nearly always thicker than the culms they produce and support, as they must support the top-heavy clump and store food reserves for times of stress.

Runners

The large group of temperate bamboos not confined to the montane regions mostly have potentially aggressive rhizome systems. From the many different genera in this category, *Phyllostachys* and *Sasa* are two good examples. Running rhizomes are rounded with elongated segments (internodes) separating the nodes. This type of rhizome also has a terminal bud which continues to extend the rhizome outwards until it produces a new culm. At the same time, it can produce a secondary or lateral bud which develops the rhizome, allowing it to grow vigorously outwards. To further elaborate on the difference between clumping and running rhizome systems, the distance between individual culms above ground on some of the more aggressive species, especially on mature plants, can be up to fifty times that of those produced from a clumping type.

The culms that are produced are nearly always thicker than the rhizomes they appear from, so as the rhizome thickens and becomes more extensive in the

↑ An aggressive *Phyllostachys aureosulcata*. This plant does not usually spread but as the soil is dry here, the bamboo has been forced to go in search of moisture

↑ Although vigorous and speedy, *Chusquea gigantea* is not classed as invasive

ground, the culm structure above ground will also become more robust in girth and height. A running bamboo in its native habitat forms extensive groves sometimes extending a few metres in a year, but brought into a cooler garden this invasive quality is often lessened. When this restrictive habit occurs, it could also fall into the following category due to its changed habit.

The in-betweens

This type of rhizome system can be said to be intermediate in structure, falling between those of clumping and running types. For example, two specific types of the clumping or pachymorph rhizome system, namely *Chusquea* and *Yushania*, produce culms that will spread more widely than those of an average clumping type, but these plants have a strong capacity to produce a vigourous,

mature plant quickly. These two genera are noted for forming longer necks between the bulbous rhizomes and producing wider spaced culms, which therefore creates a wider diameter at the base of the plant more quickly than other clumping types would. Though never aggressive, *Chusquea* is well noted for its wider spacing between culms.

Yushania species are also more open in habit with slightly longer rhizome necks, but instead of spaced individual culms, they have separated clusters of tightly packed culms of varying thickness. This habit is quite unique, as at the very base of the main culm, the rhizomes can produce new buds from which secondary culms emerge. This formation is known as tillering. This intermediate rhizome type is also seen in the short *Shibataea* species and the taller forms of the Japanese *Pleioblastus*.

↑ A colourful culm of *Yushania maculata*

↑ The colourful new shoots of *Phyllostachys iridescens* will grow upwards to head height in just a few days

Above Ground

Although bamboos' underground systems have an effect on their various types and appearances, it is mainly for ornamental reasons that we plant them. Although not as complicated as the rhizome structure, the development of bamboos' above ground parts is much more interesting to see. Culms first appear from pointed buds that emerge from the underground rhizome, then in a matter of weeks the branches and leaves will form as the culm expands upwards. There are some intriguing features attached to these parts that can affect the ornamental merits of an individual species. Although the terms sulci, geniculation and sheathing may not be common in general plant descriptions, these peculiarities provide unusual charms and colourings amongst the bamboo group and will be explained later.

Culms and branches

The jointed culms arising from the rhizomes can vary widely in thickness. On the compact *Fargesia* species, the culms rarely exceed 2.5 cm (1 in.) in diameter and produce a range of bamboos from 2 m to 5 m (6.5 ft. to 16. 5 ft.) in height. The ground cover forms can have culms as thin as 0.3 cm (0.15 in.) in diameter, as with 'Pygmy Bamboo' (*Pleioblastus pygmaeus*), which only reaches 30 cm (1 ft.) in height. On many of the giant *Phyllostachys*, culm girth on a mature plant averages 8 cm (3 in.), but can measure 18 cm (7 in.) in warmer, sheltered gardens with long summers, given plenty of moisture. As a general rule, bamboos with thinner culms produce plants that are much shorter in stature than those with thicker culms. It is worth repeating at this point that giant bamboos need an extensive colony of rhizomes to support their great height and weight, not forgetting also that many

↑ A varied selection of bamboo culms

↑ A new shoot of *Phyllostachys aureosulcata* f. *aureocaulis*

of the very short forms of bamboo can be quite aggressive in their colonisation due to the nature of their probing rhizome systems. The clump formers always achieve average height between the two tall and short extremes, and as such produce average or medium sized culms.

Culms of temperate bamboos grow very quickly only during the warmer months and reach full height in approximately six to twelve weeks, depending on the exact weather conditions at the time. For example, if a cool, dry spell occurs during their period of growth, their rate of growth may slow and their potential culm height may reduce. An unbroken period of warmth and humidity will have the opposite effect, allowing the culms to reach their full development. Just like with true grasses, the thickness of a bamboo culm will remain the same throughout its life, while similarly the height a bamboo reaches in a single growing season is the height at which the bamboo will remain for its entire life. The life

expectancy of culms varies depending on the genera and species, but as a general rule, the more mature the bamboo the longer the individual culms will live (but also be continually replaced). A young, juvenile bamboo with thin culms will develop over a period of time into maturity and as it does, the original thin culms will die out naturally as energy is diverted towards the stronger growth. On a thin, juvenile plant, original culms may only last two or three years. Any culms that naturally die out should be removed by cutting them at ground level to keep the plant tidy.

Each species of bamboo has its own particular shooting time in temperate gardens, but in the northern hemisphere this is normally from late March to early August. If the bamboo originates from a northern location (or one with a high-altitude), it usually shoots in early spring, because growth has to start earlier in these cooler locations to allow time for the culms to fully develop and for the new rhizomes to become active before the onset of cooler

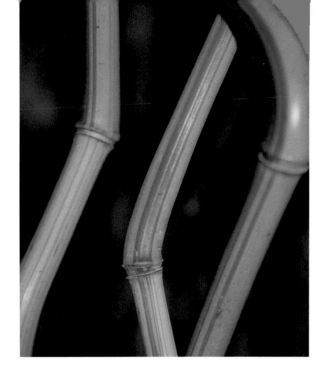

↑ Geniculation (zigzag shaping) on culms of *Phyllostachys aureosulcata* 'Argus'

weather. Conversely, bamboos that come from the warmer temperate regions tend to shoot at the peak of summer warmth during the longer growth season. Early shooters also tend to produce plenty of culms annually, whereas late shooting forms produce much fewer, making them slow to mature in many cases.

Unusual culms are produced on some species of bamboos – while most can't be explained, they will impress your friends! Apart from the various culm colourings, there are geniculations, congestions and swellings which all occur naturally. Geniculation is the zigzag shaping of occasional culms on some species of *Phyllostachys*, in particular the species *Phyllostachys aureosulcata* and its forms, although it can occur on other species but not as predominantly. This kinking always begins near the base of the culm, usually no more than 1 m (3 ft.) from the ground. The culm turns to an angle of approximately 45 degrees from vertical, then it grows back on itself 90 degrees before turning upwards again to vertical by

another 45 degrees, all in the space of two or three days. *Phyllostachys aurea* and its forms are also noted for their congestion of internodes and angled nodes lower down on some of the culms, thus producing a tortoiseshell effect. *Pseudosasa japonica* 'Tsutsumiana' shows bulbous swellings at the lower part of each internode on mature culms, hence its common name, Green Onion Bamboo. As well as these unusual offerings, many other bamboos show pronounced or distorted nodes, *Chimonobambusa tumidissinoda* being the best example with its saucer-like swellings.

Branches develop from buds at the solid culm nodes and are produced higher on taller and more mature culms than on young, juvenile plants. The number of branches varies within the different genera and is one of the key features of their botanical identification. Branches are also responsible for producing a sulcus or groove on some culms, specifically on *Phyllostachys* and very occasionally on *Semiarundaria*. This groove is an indent formed by the bud at the node and on *Phyllostachys* is often a different colour to the rest of the culm.

Leaf and sheath

Technically, there are two types of leaves on bamboos, although each appear at nodal segments both above and below ground. For simplicity, the average bamboophile normally uses the terms "leaf" and "sheath" to differentiate between the two leaf types. A leaf on a bamboo is basically a formation of two main parts, the sheath and the blade.

Sheaths protect the new rhizome and culm growth, with those sheaths surrounding the rhizomes rotting quickly in the soil after doing their job. Sheaths are usually very smooth on the inside to allow for the speedy growth of the rhizomes and culms. The young, emerging culms are also often coated in a fine talcum-like powder to enhance their rapid development. Being fairly rigid in their structure, the sheaths guide the culm upwards and give it support.

↑ Bamboo leaves can vary considerably according to genus

↑ A loosening sheath on a new culm of *Semiarundinaria fastuosa*

Their rough and often bristly exterior also protects against the elements and pest damage. Sheaths are attached to the solid nodes at the bamboo's base and also protect the developing buds on each node that later form branches, although some lower buds do remain dormant as branching does not occur close to ground level on most mature bamboos. The sheaths that envelop the growing culms are often very colourful, with staining and blotches of different colours on them according to their species. This is particularly evident on *Phyllostachys* species and is one of the best tools for identification. Initially, as the sheath becomes visible after emerging from the shoot, it will be either entirely green or lightly coloured and will also be able to photosynthesize, thus helping to feed the plant.

If a cross-section of a new shoot is examined, it will show a tightly compressed sequence of rings, each alternate ring being either a sheath or a culm section. As the culm grows upwards, the lower sheaths lose their colour and turn silver or pale yellow. At this point, on some genera the sheaths will fall off the culms, but on others they will persist on the culm for many years, providing an almost striped culm effect. *Pseudosasa japonica* (Arrow Bamboo) is a good example of this.

The true leaves, or blades, as we recognize them, are the main absorbers of sunlight on the branches. This energy is used to produce carbohydrates from the water being taken in by the roots and the carbon dioxide that is absorbed from the air. These leaves are attached to the branch by a narrow sheath that wraps around the branch tightly and connects to the branch nodes at the base of the plant. There is also a short flexible joint (petiole) that connects the leaf to the sheath and allows the leaves to be flexible in the wind and to find correct angle for making the most of the sunlight.

↑ The sheath blades at the tip of a new shoot of *Phyllostachys iridescens*

↑ The heavily veined leaves of *Sasa palmata* f. *nebulosa* also boast invisible, tessellated cross-veining

The fine and delicate appearance of bamboo leaves belies their actual hardiness and complex appearance. On most bamboo leaves, the veins create a rectangular geometrical pattern called tessellation, which is often visible on many of the large leafed bamboos. Tessellation provides the leaves with structural reinforcement and keeps them turgid during times of drought, extreme cold and strong wind. Bamboo leaves are also continually replaced, as with all other evergreen plants. For example, *Phyllostachys* species lose a portion of their oldest leaves at shooting time in spring and summer so that the plant's energy can be partly preserved for the speedy shoot emergence. In contrast, *Fargesia* species shed some of their leaves during late autumn or early winter, mimicking this same occurrence in their natural habitat. They are lightening their load to reduce possible desiccation before the onset of a harsh winter. It is worth mentioning that this leaf loss occurs during a period of only two or three weeks and for the rest of the year the bamboos look very fresh.

Also, bamboos' fallen leaves and sheaths are in fact the best food and mulch for the developing plants and should always be left where they fall at the base of the plant. As they rot down, they provide the correct balance of nutrients in the soil, as well as keeping moisture in the soil and suppressing weed growth.

In Your Garden

↑ Interesting combinations in a small place

Right Plant, Right Place – Where to Put Your Bamboo

Irrespective of whether you have a large garden estate, small urban spot or a tiny balcony, there will be a bamboo that is suitable for your space. Planning and designing a garden is a similar process to checking a list of ingredients for a recipe and running your eye over the method. Gardening can be as simple as creating a colour scheme, selecting forms and textures and putting a few plants together to create a year round feature in your garden. Endless possibilities arise when you're using natural and man-made landscaping materials and softening the architecture with some sympathetic planting. Alternatively, you could just need one bamboo in a particular place to finish the space to your liking. Of course, there are also bamboo gardens – these are normally large in scale and comprise of a collection of individually spaced plants to showcase all their forms and habits. These are generally created by truly addicted enthusiasts.

However, nearly all gardeners that are trying bamboos for the first time just want to incorporate a plant or two into their gardens to try something new, or they might indeed have a specific need for the bamboo to fulfil. Like all plants in a garden, a bamboo must be worthy of its allotted space. This is especially true in a small garden, when everything is always under close observation.

When making a selection there are many considerations to take into account, such as the bamboo's ultimate height, length of time to maturity and whether it is invasive, clumping or variable, depending on your location. As well as the crucial points above, there are many more frequently asked questions about bamboos, about their different uses and locations in the garden. Hopefully, the plant

descriptions featured later in this book will give you some ideas and answer some of your questions about using bamboos. In the meantime, here are a few more suggestions, guidelines and reminders to help you succeed.

↑ *Phyllostachys* leaves with backlighting

Small Gardens

Making good use of all available space in a small garden is vital, as is the need for careful plant selection. Every plant will be looked at more closely here, whether it is pleasing to the eye or not. One of the things I am often asked for when discussing small gardens are very tall but not spreading bamboos (those over 6 m (20 ft.) or more in ultimate height) to

↑ The exotic effect viewed from indoors. Palms and *Phormium* mix effectively with *Sasa palmata* f. *nebulosa* (left) and a golden *Phyllostachys* (right)

↑ *Phyllostachys aureosulcata* 'Lama Tempel' amongst lower plants in a small front garden

use for screening from neighbours' windows. I must say firmly at this point that this request is usually near on impossible, because a bamboo of great height needs broad support from below. However, there are some good clumping bamboos that can reach 5 m (16.5 ft.) with careful placement and are more suited to the job. Some are also light and airy in leaf, casting less shadow but still providing the interruption of view from next door. Their delicate growth also makes a better contrast to other plants.

Helpful hints

- Use clumping forms such as *Borinda*, *Fargesia* and *Thamnocalamus*.
- The straight and upright forms of *Phyllostachys* are

very good for narrow borders or gardens.
- Avoid the very tall and usually aggressive, unless you can safely contain them by barriers (see page 157) and maintain them frequently.
- Bear in mind that the shade that bamboos cast may affect you or your neighbours.
- Avoid very weeping habits, unless the bamboo is short and suited to trimming (*Fargesia rufa* is one such example). Taller weeping forms will intrude into your airspace, or if planted by a boundary will hang over the neighbouring garden. Taller forms with arching foliage are better by a path, as their vertical structure will hold the foliage high over head.
- Make sure that any invasive bamboos are contained or controlled, or they will escape

rapidly into other plants' space and under shallow foundations and paths, only to appear on the other side. Larger invasive bamboos can also cause damage to old and shallow wall foundations, although modern structures are usually stronger.

- Be aware of where your plumbing and cables are. While modern utilities are deep enough not to be damaged, access to them may be impeded by any substantial planting above.
- Use medium height bamboos for screening compost heaps, bins and other unsightly structures.
- Shorter bamboos such as *Shibataea* or *Indocalamus tessellatus* will be fine in the soil because they are more easily controlled, but others are best in pots on hard landscaping.
- Tall bamboos can add another dimension in an otherwise confined space full of shorter plants. Even by just using these in the background, you can create the feeling of privacy and enclosure.
- The taller the bamboo, the closer other plants can be planted without taking away their natural beauty.

Specimen Planting

In gardening terms, the word specimen is often used when a plant is required as a stand-alone structure. Any bamboo can be planted in isolation, but when specimen planting a choice is nearly always made due to a desire for architectural value or a focal point within the rest of the garden. Whatever is chosen, make sure the solitary bamboo is worthy of its space.

Helpful hints

- Remove turf when planting in lawns or grassland to allow for better establishment of a young bamboo. The grass can be allowed to grow again once the bamboo is established, as the bamboo will simply grow through the grass. Bear in mind that bamboos shed leaves and sheaths at various times

according the type planted, so make sure fallen leaves and sheaths are raked off the turf and put closely around the base of a young bamboo. This litter will not only help to mulch the bamboo and conserve moisture, but will also provide nutrients as it decays. On mature plants, more spent leaves will be produced than can be used around the bamboo, so clear them away regularly for tidiness and to also benefit the turf.

- The colourful timber bamboos of the *Phyllostachys* group, along with *Chusquea* specimens, will provide the boldest of statements, but large spaces are needed for these. For smaller areas, if you wish to have some lawn left after a few years, choose the taller forms of *Fargesia*.
- Take the background into account. A bamboo that has a similar shape or colouring to something behind it will not stand out.

↓ A solitary specimen of *Phyllostachys vivax* f. *aureocaulis*

↑ The beauty of a *Phyllostachys nigra*
is focussed by the effective lighting

- Weeping bamboos require more room to act
  as a solitary statement, so in a lawn area their
  overhanging branches may be a nuisance when
  cutting grass.
- A feature plant will always be up for inspection,
  so make sure you know the best way to keep the
  bamboo in good shape. With *Phyllostachys* for
  example, the removal of older and thinner culms
  (and on some species, removal of low branches) is
  always best done in winter.
- A root barrier is advisable, but ensure that you
  leave enough space for future root growth.

Association, Mixed Borders and Materials

I have always believed that bamboos are just as
versatile as many other garden plants, and when
used in the right combination, a simple grouping
of just a few individuals can become a work of art.
Combining colours, textures and shapes, with or
without materials is also just as important as the
plants themselves. In terms of association, you are
only limited to the huge range of ornamental garden
plants and materials that are available.

Perhaps the main choice to make when mixing
bamboos with other plants is selecting which one will
be the feature plant. It is easy to use a bamboo as the
dominant plant, but in fact there are many bamboos
that can be used as suitable foils for small trees and
large shrubs.

↑ A mixed planting of bamboo with winter shrubs and a simple cobbled path joining two parts of a small garden

↑ Purely bamboos. From left to right: *Sasa palmata* f. *nebulosa, Phyllostachys nuda* and *Pleioblastus shibuyanus* 'Tsuboi'

Helpful hints

- If you are new to gardening, use tried and tested plants. The bamboos in this book certainly are, but don't shy away from common plants in other plant groups as these are nearly all long-lived and reliable. Some newer hybrids may look exciting, however some can be finicky with their needs and often do not have the strength of their parents.

- Use different shapes. A tall feature bamboo with a stiff culm structure can be complemented by balled, domed and fountain shapes in associated planting. Horizontal and layered plants also work well with tall bamboos as they accentuate the perpendicular.

- Leaf size and texture can also be a key to success. Fine and delicate bamboo leaves can be offset by the bold and brash leafage of many popular, exotic looking plants with great effect, such as the woody and hardy Palms, *Chamaerops* and *Trachycarpus* or *Hosta* 'Sum and Substance', *Trachystemon orientalis* and *Acanthus mollis* for their lush foliage displays.

- Make sure you know the habit and vigour of each plant you are using. Plant too closely and some could be spoiled by close proximity, usually by shade or competition for nutrients and water. Good spacing also allows each plant to best display its wares and also makes moving them in later years easier when space could be required.

- Features such as paths, patios, decking and fencing can be softened using bamboos as their soft branching and leaves will distract from the harsh lines and edges of the structures.
- Bamboos are enhanced by an unfussy background such as a wall, fence or dark conifer hedge.
- Choose wisely in small gardens, as every plant here has an important role to play, while larger gardens are more forgiving of mistakes. If you are fortunate enough to have the space, then try planting three or more of a kind. This can be most effective when viewed from afar.
- Avoid spreading bamboos in small planting areas, as they will quickly smother any adjacent lesser plants unless you can control them.
- Don't forget that most bamboos are evergreen and have year round value. Their greenery or variegation is a foil for just about anything. When thinking about colours of other plants, take their winter brightness into account so that there will always be something of interest in your garden apart from the bamboo.

The Bamboo Garden

Usually only associated with serious bamboo enthusiasts, bamboo gardens are nearly always grand in scale. To collect them in large variety and allow them to grow to mature dimensions, you will need at least a few acres for an effective display of well-spaced individual specimens. However, with many more (particularly clumping) species becoming available, it is possible to create a lesser but just as effective collection in a smaller plot.

Helpful hints
- Make sure each bamboo has enough space to display its individual habit and charms. Bamboos that grow into each other with delving rhizome systems are very difficult to separate.

↑ These two bamboos have been given enough room to fully develop without competition

- Mix up the lower forms amongst the tall ones, the large leaved varieties between the less exotic and the colours amongst the greens. This will create a random but undulating mass of billowing greenery from a distance, but up close each bamboo's individual characteristics will be accentuated by those of a very different neighbour.
- The use of meandering pathways around islands of bamboo (creating a maze-like effect) can be more effective than the formality of planting in straight lines. Unless they are edging a driveway or screening a boundary, large groupings of bamboos do not lend themselves to formality.
- In a small to medium plot, think about using the maximum number of colours, leaf sizes, height and habits that your garden will allow, to create the illusion of a collection. Avoid the very invasive where possible to save you much work and frustration. Underplanting timber bamboos

with shorter ground cover ones is also a way of increasing the number of bamboos in a small space.

- Whatever size your bamboo garden is, try to think long term and ensure there is either a lot of space or a barrier of some sort between each bamboo.

Waterside Planting

Regardless of whether you have a tiny pond, a small lake or garden by a river, there is nothing more beautiful than the reflection of a bamboo to further accentuate its form and highlight its evergreen beauty. Waterside bamboos are more effective if isolated and not congested by other woody or taller reed-like plants. Framed by the background or distant horizon with sunlight behind, the foliage will cast its imagery onto the water. Sit yourself nearby for times of restful tranquillity and contemplation.

Helpful hints

- If your pond is lined with a manufactured butyl rubber material or even clay, be careful that the sharp, penetrating rhizomes and buds do not penetrate this and create leaks, which would be difficult to repair. Either put in a clumping *Fargesia* or *Thamnocalamus*, install a rhizome barrier or plant far enough away from the edge of the water that it will take the bamboo many years to get there.
- If your pond is natural or fed by a spring, make sure you are aware of the highest level the water can reach. Although an established bamboo can tolerate its feet in water for periods of up to two months, it will not survive in permanently waterlogged conditions.
- Bamboos also can be useful in the foreground against larger stretches of water. The tall, well-spaced culm structure of the timber-like *Phyllostachys* will allow water still to be seen.
- Weeping bamboos such as *Fargesia utilis*, *Fargesia*

↑ Although on a grand scale, these bamboos offer a useful reflective quality and soften the hard landscape

rufa, and *Fargesia murielae* are ideal at the side or back of a pond, with their cascades of greenery pointing downwards towards the waterside.

- Ground cover bamboos and medium height spreaders are useful for binding and stabilizing the banks of large natural ponds and rivers, helping to prevent erosion. Because of their matted interwoven rhizome structure, they are more tolerant of flooding than individual specimen bamboos. Parts of the rhizome above the water level will be able to breathe and support the rest of the submerged rhizome.
- Although evergreen, the bamboos will shed some leaves and sheaths, either when new growth starts in spring, just before winter or in times of severe drought, depending on the genus and species planted. Although this will have no detrimental effect on the water quality, it is best to remove them from the water surface if possible, particularly

on smaller water features. The leaves are not poisonous to fish and other aquatic life.

- Water is a natural root barrier to the bamboos.

Wild and Woodland

The natural beauty of a deciduous woodland or large semi-wild garden can be good enough for many people. However, during the seemingly endless winter season, punctuating bare trees and bushes with bamboos is a way of lifting the gloom, providing a more solid framework and a haven for wildlife at all times of year. Any evergreen planting is not only useful for game birds but also for general wildlife, providing warm shelter in winter and a safe haven for nesting in spring. Bamboos have the ability to bring a woodland to life, with their culms and branches rustling in the wind, combined with the chattering of birds at dawn and before nightfall.

↑ A narrow path surrounded by vigorous bamboos under overhanging trees

Helpful hints

- If possible, keep grass and scrub cleared away from an area that is to be planted with bamboo for at least two years. This will allow for better establishment.
- Mulch around the bamboo to prevent moisture loss, especially when access to water is limited. Mulching will also help to reduce weed growth around the base of the bamboo, cutting down on the competition. When planting, also use young stock that requires less water, as a large specimen from a container or garden division will need much more attention to keep it moist and stable in the freshly cultivated soil.
- Plant in clearings where possible, preferably with some dappled overhead light so the greenery can glow in the dim woodland. If planted too close to the roots of a large tree, the bamboo will suffer from drought because of the dominance of the larger plant.

- Be aware that in wilder areas there can be a prevalence of larger wildlife, ranging from rabbits to deer. Most will not have an effect on a mature, established bamboo but a deer can decimate a young plant in just one sitting. Protect young plants with netting or mesh fencing. Gophers, badgers, voles, squirrels, rats and moles can also disturb young, newly planted bamboos below ground and make the root and rhizome vulnerable to drying out.
- Bamboos with coloured culms (other than the green and the variegated forms) are well suited to the darker surrounds and offer welcome interest all year round.
- In large woodlands, many of the more invasive and vigorous bamboos can be used to grand effect.

↑ Almost a wilderness

↑ *Indocalamus tessellatus* as
ground cover underneath mixed
Phyllostachys bambusoides
'Castillonis' and 'Castillonis Inversa'

Ground Cover

In a gardening sense, the term ground cover nearly always applies to short plants that carpet the ground either in colonies, such as bamboos, grasses or perennials, or from a central woody crown such as a spreading juniper. Other criteria for ground cover usually describe quick growing plants that can cover the ground efficiently, are low maintenance and provide ornamental value. Shorter bamboos meet all of these requirements with ease.

Helpful hints

- Any form of ground cover planting has the benefit of suppressing potential weed growth and stabilising the soil. Gradual decay of old leaves and sheaths from bamboos will also increase the organic content and nutrients in the soil. There are more advantages than disadvantages regarding this low infill type, as the only other alternatives are bare earth or a form of mulch, such as bark or shingle.

- The living carpet of short bamboo has to be considered competition for any surrounding plants. If planning and planting an entire area, make sure the underplanting is far enough away to allow the other plants to establish without initial competition. On borders with bare soil between already established plants, competition is not such a problem, but more watering may be necessary to establish the ground cover.

- Do not forget that most short bamboos are invasive, which is not a concern in very large borders. In a small border, be aware that growth can extend from the soil into a lawn, under a fence, patio, path or entwine into the neighbouring roots of a favoured plant. Use solid boundaries to

↑ *Sasa veitchii* is one of the finest bamboos for ground cover

Screening, Hedging and Windbreaks

As well as being excellent for general screening and hedging, bamboos have a few more important qualities. They provide filtering and protection from the wind and are also barriers against noise. Their almost constant movement with rustling branches and flickering leaves offers a welcome distraction from the hum of everyday life beyond the garden. Bamboos are a valuable sanctuary for birdlife, both in the cold and at night. They also have less formality than some of the more traditional hedging and can provide an airy and relaxed atmosphere, but are still imposing and distinctive.

Requests for plants that can be used for impenetrable screening and boundary planting are frequent and well known to many growers. The previous fashion of using the ubiquitous and formal Leyland cypress (×*Cupressocyparis leylandii*) is now regretted by many gardeners, especially those with small gardens. Although undoubtedly fast, this conifer is high maintenance and requires quite a bit of room and work to keep it in check and make it suitable for formal hedging. It is also greedy at the root and impoverishing to the soil. Before this, the cherry laurel (*Prunus laurocerasus*) was widely used. This is also fast but again requires much room, though it is easier to maintain and able to regenerate from the hardest of pruning. Bamboo is often used as a replacement for these after their owners have razed them to the ground.

Helpful hints

- As has been mentioned before, the size of your garden relates very much to what you should plant. In large gardens, there are obviously fewer limitations as to what you can use, but in small gardens use clump forming bamboos or be prepared to restrict and contain the growth of more vigorous forms.

narrow or confine the space, such as thick timber or concrete kerbing.
- Many of the suitable ground cover bamboos are as good in half shade as they are in full sun. Once established, the short *Pleioblastus* and low *Sasa veitchii* can be kept lush, neat and showy by shearing to the ground annually in late winter.
- There are few other plants more tolerant of living underneath tree canopies than bamboos. However, because of the moisture used by the trees in summer, additional watering of the surrounding plants may be needed.
- Always bear plant association in mind. Make sure harmony is created by using different colours, structures and foliage effects to contrast with the feature plants, punctuating the carpeting below.

↑ *Phyllostachys* hedging alongside a narrow border offers privacy and cool shade to the glass-fronted conservatory

↑ *Phyllostachys vivax* as a partition between two properties

- If replacing an already established hedge with bamboo, you will have to consider how to remove the leftover stumps and roots. This particularly applies to small gardens where there is less room, as planting through a woody root system will prove almost impossible. In larger gardens, it may be possible to plant on either side of the existing root system, or allow the new bamboo hedge to develop before removal of the old hedge. The further away the existing roots are from the new bamboo the better, as this will allow for quick establishment of the new plants. This is because soil close to the base of an old hedge is nearly always dry and infertile.

- Spacing bamboos for screens and hedges is dependent on a few important factors. When planting a hedge of bamboos of the same species, form or cultivar, or even a mixed hedge with bamboos of equal vigour, technically you can plant them as close together as you like. The plants will eventually merge together as if they were one, so the closer you plant, the quicker the immediate screen will be created. But be warned – the issue with close proximity planting is that even bamboos that look identical in appearance and potential vigour at time of purchase can have slight variations in the strengths of their rhizomes and bud quantity. There are almost always a few plants that don't quite keep up with the rest.

- For mixed bamboo hedges and screenings where many different genera and forms are used, every plant will have its own speed of maturity and will require its own space to establish itself. A minimum of 1 m (3.3 ft.) is the optimum spacing between plants to allow for their reliable establishment, though it is possible to plant clumping kinds

↑ A perfectly trimmed bamboo hedge in a subtropical environment

slightly closer together while very vigorous specimens should be planted further apart. It is better to stagger the plants if you wish to plant them in a double row, as this helps to cover any gaps but also requires similar spacing to the first line of hedging.

- Border and planting width also has to be considered, especially in small to medium sized gardens. A bamboo will not grow in any one particular direction, as they usually merely expand outwards in every direction from the original planting. If it is capable of growing 1 m (3.3 ft.) along the length of the hedge, then it will undoubtedly grow to the same dimension in terms of its width. The only way to force a bamboo sideways is to contain its width, which means containing it with barriers or kerbing to force it sideways. Too much restriction (especially of tall and vigorous bamboos) will compromise their vigour and the final height and appearance of the plants. As a compromise, put a barrier at the rear of the hedge, which will stop the bamboo from exceeding its boundary. As most hedges and screens need height for privacy and protection, select the taller clumping kinds for these.

- It is possible to create a solid or shaped hedge effect by using selective trimming with single species screens and hedges. Species that have dense branch systems such as *Fargesia*, *Pseudosasa* and *Phyllostachys aurea* (and forms), can all be pruned. This is best done during midsummer in cooler areas (with secateurs and loppers for the branches) and during late autumn when reducing the height of the ripened culms. In warmer climates, it is possible to use shears and hedgetrimmers for trimming due to the longer growing season in these areas, as recovery from the cutting will be quicker.

- Mixed bamboo hedging is far less formal than single species hedging – the different textures, colours, forms and variations in height will create a pleasing and unique cloudscape effect. This type of hedging is more appreciated in medium sized gardens, when it is used as a feature rather than just a background.

- Single species hedging and screening is quite formal and best used in large gardens as a background to more ornamental planting. When trying this, use green culmed bamboos and bring the more colourful ornamental forms into prominence in the garden. Also, if a single species flowers and suffers as a result, then the entire hedge will do likewise. This should be a good enough reason to persuade you to use a mixture of species.

- Short hedging (below head height) can be used as partitions and for edging, but when attempting this use clumping forms or contain the roots as they can be very invasive. Many of the shorter bamboos have a dense branch system that makes them suitable for light trimming.

Pots and Containers

Many books have been written about the art of container gardening, as technically almost any plant can be grown in a pot with a little care and skill. But remember, growing plants in containers places them in an artificial environment, as pots do not exist in the wild or natural landscape. Having said that, there are many positives to growing bamboos in pots. They can be moved around easily to create a new look in the garden, combined easily for plant association and some of the more invasive kinds can be kept within bounds. In fact, bamboos can look quite superb when properly cared for in pots. The different styles, colours and shapes of the bamboos and their pots set an exciting challenge for all gardeners, including skilled gardeners or perfectionists.

Helpful hints

Balance

- Without the rigid support and grip that the earth provides, bamboos in pots may be unstable. The balance or equilibrium between a pot and its plant is thus critical. To keep the plant upright in the wind, the centre of gravity must be low in terms of the plant and pot unit. A tall plant in a narrow pot with little basal contact on the ground will blow over in the slightest breeze. For tall bamboos especially, stable pots and compost are required. These will help to create the balance needed to keep your bamboo upright.

Pot type

- Selecting pots for bamboos is a veritable minefield for every beginner. An expensive pot is usually either very ornate or of the best quality. The best you could have would be a very thick and heavily

↑ *Phyllostachys aureosulcata* f. *spectabilis* (centre), flanked by *Fargesia murielae* 'Bimbo' (left), *Fargesia rufa* and *Indocalamus tessellatus* (right), with assorted evergreens

structured, kiln-fired and glazed ceramic container – these are nearly always frost-proof and can last a lifetime. Plastic is also good and relatively inexpensive – the best choices are pots that are less brittle, which will last at least a decade or so. Timber containers are not as long lasting unless thick and well treated with a preservative, but they are usually very effective in terms of their natural qualities and appearance. Another advantage with timber is that you can construct your own container. Concrete containers are useful and usually substantial and weighty, though after a few years they will likely become weathered. The only type of container I would avoid is terracotta, which soaks up moisture and is nearly always unglazed, making it susceptible to damage in hard frosts. It is also possible for pot-bound rhizome systems to crack terracotta pots when expanding, as these pots are more brittle than glazed ceramic ones.

- One more important point – never "over pot" a bamboo (or any other plant for that matter). In other words, do not put the smallest of plants in the largest of tubs as it will simply not be able to breathe or cope and will wallow in the cold, wet compost. When potting a plant, it is better to choose a pot that is one or two sizes up than the previous one each time, as that way the bamboo roots and rhizomes can travel quickly to the sides of the new pot for warmth and air.

- Pot shape is also important. The stability problems that can arise using narrow containers were mentioned earlier, but these also apply to any pots that are taller than they are wide (particularly those with an open v-shape in which the weight will be too high in the pot). A container that is at least as wide as it is high (or preferably wider), with a large area of ground contact at the base is ideal. Avoid bulbous and barrel-like pots, or ones that curve inwards towards a narrower rim, as these shapes make the removal of a congested root-ball almost impossible. If you do use barrel-shaped pots, then grow the plant in a cheap plastic pot which can be fitted through the rim of the barrel-shaped one so it can be easily removed. Pots also need drainage holes as bamboos will not survive in waterlogged conditions.

Compost and fertilizer

- Having selected a bamboo and a pot, next comes the compost to grow the bamboo in and the fertilizer to feed it with. There are, rather dauntingly, hundreds of brands and types to choose from, which can be more than confusing for a beginner. If you have grown any outdoor plants in pots successfully before, then I'm sure the bamboo will do just as well in whatever mix you have used previously. Failing that, ask your bamboo grower for advice at the time of purchase. My own preference is to make a fifty-fifty mix of heavy loam-based compost (such as John Innes Number Three) with a general or multipurpose mixture. When buying a multipurpose mix, choose one that is good quality (usually more expensive), as it will be coarser in texture, allowing for drainage and aeration of the growing plant. If you live in an area with alkaline hard water (chalky) and water your plants using this water, make sure you start with an ericaceous mix (always clearly labelled) or your plants will soon turn yellow. Add to the half-and-half mix about ten per cent medium grade bark chippings, which will provide more drainage and a similar amount of washed coarse grit for extra ballast in the pot. Before adding the fertilizer, you will need to work out either the volume of the pot in gallons, litres or sometimes the cubic capacity. Then mix in a slow-release nitrogen fertilizer at the rate recommended for that particular product. Amounts do vary according to brand so read the instructions on the packet carefully. In subsequent years you can use a liquid fertilizer, these are usually diluted from a stronger liquid solution or powder. Feed your bamboo this solution every few weeks (or as recommended) but only during the growing season from mid-spring to early autumn. Avoid any seaweed or fish based fertilizers, as although this has not yet been proven, there have been reports that some bamboos can react unfavourably to these.

Watering

- Watering your bamboos in pots might seem like the simplest of tasks, but trust me, it isn't. Firstly, a plant only needs watering when it actually requires water. I am really trying not to insult you with that simple statement, but you would be surprised how many people water plants by routine, even when they are already wet at the roots. There is no easy way of telling you how often to water your bamboo except that you should only do so when the bamboo needs it, which is something you will have to gauge yourself. As an example, at the height of the growing season on a hot and breezy summer day, a well established bamboo in a pot may require watering twice a day, while a less established or smaller plant might only need to be watered once. In general, the bigger and more established the plant, the more water it will need. At the start of the spring, your pot may only need watering once in a week. As a general rule, use the weight of the container to get an indication as to whether it needs watering. If the pot is dry (light) the bamboo may need watering, but if it is wet (heavy) it may not. Also check the surface of the compost for any change in colour or shrinkage away from the side of the pot, as these are nearly always signs of drying out. Covering the surface of the compost with grit or similar may look very nice but it doesn't help with detecting the moisture level in the pot. When you become more confident with the watering regime, then this can be done.

Positioning

- The best situation for a young potted bamboo is a sheltered spot out of the wind to allow it to establish without having to battle the elements. In winter, it is also a good idea to protect the pot during hard frosts or very windy spells, to protect the rootball from freezing and the foliage from desiccating. Moving it against a sheltered wall will offer some protection, or better still move it into an unheated polythene tunnel or glasshouse – if you don't have either of these an outhouse or garage will suffice temporarily. Wrapping the pots in hessian or bubble-wrap will keep the worst of the winter cold out, and surrounding the bamboos

themselves with netting or fleece is good winter protection, particularly for new acquisitions. An established bamboo will be more tolerant of the vagaries of the weather, but in an open aspect may require more watering because of its exposure.

Aftercare

- Thinning older and thinner culms very early in the growing season will make it easier to see the new shoots as they appear. At the same time, lower branches can also be removed, again for aesthetic value and also for ease of watering and feeding. The advantage of thinning and pruning is that the need for water to support the top is reduced, which also keeps the bamboos in good shape and appearance. I must point out at this stage that nothing will live in a pot forever. Eventually the bamboo will become too congested at the root and rhizome, affecting the appearance of the top growth. There is no manner of feeding and nurturing capable of changing the appearance of a chlorotic (yellowing and starved) bamboo. What the plant needs in this case is potting into a larger sized container. However, if you are confronted with the problem of not being able to replant into a larger pot, then you have no other choice but to divide the bamboo in smaller pieces and start again.

Division

- This is the main and most successful propagation method used by growers for increasing their nursery stock. The other methods of rhizome cuttings or sections, bud and culm offsets and seed production are finicky, needing proper growing environments and much time and patience. These are always best left to the professionals. The basic rule for dividing a bamboo is never to be greedy. If you have a bamboo in need of attention and you think you can slice the rootball into four plants, then settle for two. It is better to produce

↑ Simple division using a saw

↑ A homemade timber planter successfully supporting a mixture of *Phyllostachys nigra* and *Phyllostachys aureosulcata* f. *aureocaulis*

two strong plants that will hardly be checked in growth from their harsh division, rather than four or more smaller pieces that will undoubtedly need much tender loving care to help them recover. The method of division is simple and best done just before growth commences in spring. Remove the plant from the pot and find a suitable place halfway between the culms and the diameter of the root mass. Take a strong, sharp saw and cut downwards to form two semicircular sections (assuming your pot is rounded), saw a slither from the sides off each section and a small slice from the base, in effect creating a blunted D-shape. One of the resulting pieces can be potted back into the original container with plenty of room for fresh compost, not forgetting that you will also have to find a home for the spare half. A culm or two may be weakened from this process, but simply remove

this at the base and at the same time thin out any weak growth from the centre of the crown. If the plant is quite tall, reduce the height of some of the culms. This is purely to balance out the growth above and below, making sure that the plant is adequately supported by its roots. Water immediately after division and place somewhere sheltered. On hot days, spray the foliage to help prevent excess transpiration or shrivelling of the leaves. A few weeks later, the bamboo will have started rooting into the fresh compost. It is then ready to be placed in a more prominent spot.

Difficult Places

Rather than dwell on the usually noted difficult places in the garden such as shade, dry areas and enclosed spaces, all of which have been detailed and explained regularly throughout this book, I refer here to placing of plants in unusual or challenging places which are part of a domesticated lifestyle and as such are not natural or normal garden environments.

Roof gardens

In congested urban environments it is not uncommon to see plants up high, breaking the skyline of concrete, glass and monotonous lines. Plants in this environment have to be tough and capable of adapting to the harshest of elements, most notably wind, cold winter exposure and the baking summer heat radiating from the surrounding man-made structures. Patience will be required and much effort needed in helping the plants survive and perform best in this case, as they cannot be left alone to fend for themselves forever. Regular maintenance and a watchful eye will always be necessary, very much as if the bamboos were growing in pots. When constructed carefully, the beauty of a raised residential terrace or a high urban office rest-zone can become an oasis of calm.

Helpful hints

- Firstly and very importantly, before you can consider any form of gardening above ground, you must get all the necessary materials and plants to their location.
- Elevators are obviously the most convenient way of transporting goods, while staircases are strenuous with limited manoeuvrability. For large projects, you may need to employ the use of a crane or winched structure at the side of the building. You will also have to transport the natural debris of plant material through natural loss and regular maintenance.
- Choose your bamboos wisely. Use the checklists in the main section to see if they are cold hardy, heat tolerant, suited to pots and containers and can cope with wind (described in the main text), depending on your location.

↑ *Phyllostachys* with a mixed association planting used to screen off tall buildings

- Don't use the tallest of bamboos unless you can provide them shelter from the wind. If planted directly in the soil they will blow over before they have the chance to establish, or even faster if they are in freestanding pots. The short and medium bamboos are always the best, not forgetting that there are many different structures and shapes within this group. Some have fluid, arching qualities, while others are quite rigid and firm in structure without being too tall.
- Avoid using bamboos with very large leaves, unless again you can give them protection from the wind. The leaves will shred in the almost constant wind.
- Roof gardens must have the support of the flat foundation of the roof or terrace structure below, so know your building and its materials and forms. Many foundations are strong enough to support quite large raised beds or long narrow troughs used

as edging for screening. The advantage to this is that bamboos and any other plants have a much greater area in which to grow and drying out also becomes less of a problem because a larger area can retain moisture for longer, very much like when planting on the ground. Watering will still be needed in times of drought, so some form of water storage or supply is also essential.

- The artificial plantings will need a firm growing media to support them. Heavy compost is best here or if the structure is supportive, use a mixture of best grade topsoil and good quality compost.
- Drainage of any structure used for planting is just as important as it is for pots. Most concrete flat roofs have either grids to underground piping or above ground gullies leading to gullies. These will have to be accessed to take away surplus water.
- Lastly, take good advice. Roof gardening in particular is a specialist subject with many considerations. There are specialist companies with informative brochures that can advise on what is right or wrong, and why, for your setting.

↑ A balcony is not an impediment to growing bamboo effectively

Balconies

A balcony is normally described as a balustraded platform on the outside of a building that can be accessed from an upper-floor doorway or exit, although many modern balconies have a screen of low toughened glass or Perspex from the outside world for both protection and safety. If it is attached to a two or three storey dwelling then height shouldn't be a problem, but if it is on the side of an apartment high in the sky then wind and exposure can be a problem. Bringing plants into a space that is designed for relaxation will be beneficial to many people. For some, it may also be their only chance to garden.

Many of the tips and hints here have already been mentioned in the sections for bamboos in pots and roof gardens, so please refer to those. However, there are two more important things to consider before you

make selections. Firstly, is your balcony in full sun or in shade for the bulk of the daytime? This will affect your plant choice and watering regime. Secondly, access is usually restricted to the house so always consider the transportation and storage of all things needed for container gardening, as it's unlikely in an apartment you will have a water-butt or a shed.

Indoor and conservatory

It is nearly a daily occurrence to switch on the television and see a newsreader, presenter or interviewer sitting comfortably in a studio quizzing some unsuspecting politician or celebrity. In an effort for the media station to present an upmarket or more relaxed atmosphere, plant life is often used. There you are, remote in hand watching the late evening news and the presenter links to a colleague who is sitting elsewhere with a microphone at the ready and there it is, just slightly to the side of the interviewer's shoulder – a bamboo in all its glory. I'll be brief and to the point – it's either plastic or temporarily been hired for specific effect.

I am not here to tell you that it is possible to take a hardy plant that naturally occurs in the wild into an indoor environment. A hardy plant is generally one that requires the cold of a winter dormant period, as well as other changes such as seasonal variations of temperature, humidity and light levels, which are unlikely in indoor environments. However, gardeners who have tried indoor gardening repoert that some success can be had, but you must realize that any failure you experience is purely a mistake to learn from, because if you do not try you will never know if it will work.

Helpful hints

- I don't wish to give you a list of hardy bamboos suited to indoor culture in fear of redress, although admittedly a few have been mentioned in the text, I would rather write about what not to use and why and leave the rest down to your experimentation. Avoid the very tall bamboos such a *Phyllostachys* and *Semiarundinaria*, obviously because of their height, but mainly because the new shoots that must be produced annually from the bamboo will be weak and lank, usually aborting due to the stress and eventually killing the plant. Tall plants will also need step ladders to maintain them, especially for the removal of yellowing leaves that become commonplace when grown indoors.
- Choose the coolest place possible, away from hot sunny windows. Never put them near a heater or wood stove if you want them to live beyond a few days (I know a customer who did). If possible, move the bamboos outdoors for good lengths of time. The foliage will be able to breathe properly and will be be washed by the rain. It may be worth acclimatizing them slowly, especially if there are

↑ If you can't grow bamboos indoors then view them closely from inside!

huge differences in temperature between inside and out.
- Consider all the points made in the section for bamboos in pots as these will apply to your plants. The only notable additional factor for growing bamboos indoors is their increased susceptibility to pests, so keep your eyes open and be ready with a cure if need be.
- It is possible to have a little more success in conservatories, orangeries and atriums, as the ventilation from windows provides air circulation, while the humidity from other plants and cooler temperatures will certainly be more beneficial to the bamboos. The extra natural light is also a bonus, but some shading will be required in the heat of summer.
- Lastly, the soundest advice I can provide you with was suggested to me by a customer, ironically

only a week ago. The lady in question had been asked by her father to find out which bamboos were more suited to indoor planting. After much discussion (mainly on my part) about the whys and wherefores of not growing bamboos inside, she calmly and meekly came up with the brightest of ideas for which I can take no credit whatsoever. Her suggestion was to buy three or more bamboos and have a rotation system for the plants – in other words, keep the one indoors looking its best, another outside or in a cooler environment while it recovers and another one outside in a pot, ready to replace the one indoors when it shows signs of stress. The lady also suggested that the shorter *Pleioblastus* in particular could be used because of their regenerative qualities after a hard pruning. At that point, I didn't enlighten her as to my future plans for promoting the use of indoor bamboos with the slogan "Buy Three for Success", for fear of stealing her thunder, but what I did learn is that it only takes common sense to solve a simple problem, and I intend to give this a try.

Themes and Styles

Contemporary style

Bamboos have been widely used in both old and modern styles of gardening. Pristine specimens of architectural bamboos are often seen in gardening displays at exhibitions such as the Royal Horticultural Society's Chelsea Flower Show in London, often in an imaginative or contemporary style. In modern urban environments, bamboos are fast becoming more fashionable as many architects are now accepting that plant life has an important part to play alongside modern buildings and venues. Bamboos are often seen in these sorts of environments as large individual specimens, making a bold statement or highlighting the crisp lines of some modern building. Alternatively, large swathes of smaller or ground

↑ Using just a few plants and simple materials you can create your own unique style. (Left to right: In the soil, *Phyllostachys bambusoides* 'Allgold'. In pots: *Fargesia rufa*, *Nandina domestica* 'Firepower', *Carex* 'Ice Dance' and *Indocalamus tessellatus*

↓ A fine example of contemporary gardening showing simplicity and imagination. Although the bamboos appear scorched, they are just going through a seasonal shedding and will appear fresh in a matter of weeks

cover bamboos are often used in more open-plan designs where the view must not be interrupted, including roadside plantings at junctions in towns and cities.

In contemporary styles, there is usually a mix of materials and plants, as both are as important as each other in terms of the statements they make. There are no bounds to the imagination for this style of garden design, but to get ideas I would suggest visiting modern gardens, exhibitions and just being observant of how bamboos are used in newly developed urban settings. The use of simple and easily obtained hard landscape materials such as timber, garden ornaments, stones and pebbles can add a new dimension to any garden. For one idea, just take one well shaped bamboo, with a few sea-worn large pebbles scattered at its base, add some short, vertical timber palisades at the side of the plant to frame its beauty and structure. Better still, put a flat topped timber log under the branches of a tall bamboo with a some stepping stones leading in towards it and you have a simple place for contemplation. Use two logs and you also have somewhere to place the liquid refreshment. Paving lines, vertical timber pergolas and gazebos can also be softened using smaller, arching bamboos, or accentuated further with some upright timber bamboos. Find a spot for some stone, a tasteful fountain and carefully placed night lighting or lanterns, then install some outdoor seating for the balmy summer nights and you will immediately imagine that you are in a very exotic location.

Exotic and mediterranean style

The exotic style of gardening is now very much in fashion, with gardeners seemingly willing to experiment with an endless array of subtropical flora for a summer effect. There is much work involved using these less hardy plants, because protection and some warmth must be given to keep many of them

↑ Not quite the Japanese style but modern and different. This carefully manicured *Phyllostachys aureosulcata* f. *aureocaulis* steals the limelight

alive during winter, but the bonus with bamboos is that many are completely hardy. If you haven't got the time or facilities to incorporate a seasonal planting style, be reassured that there are many other hardy plants that you can use for a similar summer effect. There are many plants with sword-like or spiky leaves that offer a contrast in form to bamboos, such as *Cordyline*, *Yucca* and *Phormium*, which are all reliably hardy. Any large leaved plant will be a foil to many smaller leaved bamboos, such as *Eucalyptus*, *Aucuba*, *Magnolia grandiflora*, *Elaeagnus*, *Catalpa*, *Fatsia* and some of the *Rhododendron* group. Conversely, many of the large leaved bamboos are excellent at associating with small leaved plants such as *Tamarix*, *Hebe*, *Cytisus*, *Azara*, *Pittosporum* and *Buxus*. I have also seen lavender, sage and rosemary planted with bamboos to good effect. All are excellent and useful additions to this southern European style.

As well as the contrast between large and small

↑ The strap-like arching leaves of
Phormium contrast well with the
tall and vertical *Phyllostachys*

leaves to create effect, there are many plants that are
often not perceived as being hardy, such as palms, but
in fact many of these species are in fact hardy. Many
of the *Trachycarpus* palms, namely the species *fortunei*,
takil and *wagnerianus*, are natives of the Himalayas
and eastern Asia and will tolerate all but the hardest
winters without damage. If you have a little more
shelter from the wind, try *Chamaerops humilis*, a palm
from the mountains of northern Africa and southwest
Europe. Other suitable candidates with the exotic
touch include *Rheum* (rhubarb), *Gunnera*, *Pseudopanax*,
broad leaved cultivars of *Miscanthus* such as 'Cabaret'
and 'Cosmopolitan' with their vivid white striped
leaves, and also one of the tallest of the species,
sacchariflorus. Tree ferns and the other low forms of

this plant group are also commonly used in the exotic
style.

Oriental style

The main reason behind this style of gardening
centres on the symbolism of nature and materials in
harmony, which ties in strongly with many eastern
religious beliefs. Bamboo is considered a friend and
a travelling companion, relating very much to the
belief that humanity cannot exist without nature
(and, by extension, bamboos). In Chinese history,
bamboo is a representation of life's path, reflecting
the endurance, elasticity and tenacity that should be
part of everyday human nature. Bamboo bends with
the wind, its leaves blow yet do not fall, it survives all
and therefore it conquers.

To successfully duplicate this almost pure style
of gardening requires much skill, learning and
understanding. To carry it off to perfection, there are
rules that must be followed. You will need to research
this style in gardens, read about the subject or join
one of the many garden societies that relate only to
Japanese or Chinese gardening. However, there is no
reason to follow the rules completely when creating
this style. A simple gravel garden with a few rocks, a
small Koi pond and some carefully selected plants,
all given their own space, can create a garden that
is highly meaningful to you. Gardening is all about
breaking the rules to produce something individual
and unique for you to enjoy. *Phyllostachys* and
Semiarundinaria are traditionally used in the Orient
as they are easily shaped and manicured, but some
of the large leaved *Indocalamus* are effective when
surrounded by gravel. A layered pine or two and
some low evergreen sedges and grasses will provide
different shapes and textures to create an air of
simplicity.

↑ A classic planting in a Chinese garden. The stately *Phyllostachys* in the corner is flanked by a *Nandina domestica* (Heavenly bamboo) (left), with grasses and a shaped pine

→ *Phyllostachys vivax* f. *aureocaulis* (right) as a background in a Japanese moss garden

50
of the best

← A patchwork of foliage

A note on using common names

Many plants do not actually have common names, including bamboos. Over the past two or three decades, many common names have been invented for bamboos (and other plants), usually with the aim of making the plant more appealing to the buyer. Many of these names describe key features of a bamboo, some are simply the cultivar names and others are abbreviated forms of the full name. When seeking out a bamboo from a nursery, it is always worth making a note of the botanical name as the average grower will most likely know the bamboos by this name.

"A wise choice for filling those wide open spaces ..."

Checklist

✗ Non-invasive
✗ Short (0.3 –1.5 m)
✗ Medium (1.5–3.5 m)
✓ **Tall (3.5 m +)**
✓ **Cold hardy**
✓ **Heat tolerant**
✓ **Drought tolerant**
✗ Moisture tolerant
✗ Pots and containers
✓ **Good for plant association**
✗ Waterside planting
✓ **Hedging, screening and windbreaks**

← A young plant of *Bashania fargesii* in winter

← A silver-grey culm of *Bashania fargesii*

Bashania fargesii
Fargesii Bamboo, Silver Cane or Silver Streak Bamboo

This has a vertical, rigid habit and forms a colony of strong silvery culms with lush verdant foliage. Makes a large open grove.

Culms: 2.5–5 cm (1–2 in.)
Leaves: 15 × 2.5 cm (6 × 1 in.)

Hardiness and aspect
Min. −25°C (−13°F), zone 5
Sun or shade.

Dimensions
Height: 5–10 m (16.5–33 ft.), average 6 m (20 ft.)
Spread: 2–10 m (6.5–33 ft.) in 10 years

Uses and combinations
Good at colonising, stabilising banks or forming large hedges and windbreaks. Foreground planting of box (*Buxus*) domes, clipped conifers, horizontal junipers or layered shrubs will enhance the verticality of this bamboo.

Although the current media fashion seems to promote plants that are compact and geared towards smaller gardens, there are still gardeners around who are blessed with plenty of space and can use many of the larger bamboos.

This Chinese native is the most common in this small genus, but deservedly so, as long as you give it the room to fulfil its promise. The bold, ghostly grey-green-silver culms rise from below ground on a speedy skyward mission during late spring. As the culms reach their full height, the branches erupt outwards, gradually turning upwards to a 45-degree angle as the leaves unfurl and align in a position to take in sunlight.

I have seen this *Bashania* in numerous locations, ranging from the driest regions to moist woodland soils. It thrives in all areas and is not in the least perturbed by extremes of exposure, drought or dim woodland gardens with frugal acid soils. In fact, the colourful culms and pale undersides of the leaves sublimely lift the gloom of a shady location. This bamboo is also slightly deeper rooted than most, helping it tolerate the driest or stoniest of ground.

A wise choice for filling those wide open spaces – after a decade or so, it can be cropped at will for garden canes or hacked through to form paths and mazes. Its overall light appearance means it associates well with other large and quick growing bamboos to form mixed screens and windbreaks, and the dark and smaller leaves on many of the equally robust *Phyllostachys* make them a worthy complement to the *Bashania*. As with many of the larger growing bamboos, this is pointless as a long-term container plant. The vigour and speedy enlargement of the rhizome system is capable of bursting plastic and cracking terracotta or ceramic at will. For containment, plant in a large raised bed, thin out the older culms regularly to avoid congestion and be prepared to supplement with water and feed during the summer months once established.

Associate planting is difficult with large bamboos as the companion plants are quickly smothered with the dominant plants' rapid development. I have used the variegated *Buxus sempervirens* 'Elegantissima', *Pinus mugo* 'Ophir' and the prostrate *Euonymus fortunei* 'Minimus', as foreground planting for the *Bashania*.

← Fresh green leaves on a young plant of *Bashania qingchengshanensis*

Look out for

Bashania qingchengshanensis, giving yourself a pat on the back if you manage to pronounce this correctly the first time! This is a relatively new introduction, equal in hardiness but perhaps with less vigour (as yet) than *B. fargesii*. This plant results in a myriad of new culms with persistent hairy sheaths that quickly produce a dense crop of new green, long lance-shaped leaves. The culms are almost solid and not as thick as its relative's, but they proudly bear the weight of the huge leaf canopy. A useful and respectably rampant foil for the coloured culm bamboos in the *Phyllostachys* group.

Borinda albocera
White Wax Borinda, Yunnan 1, 2, 3A and 3B

This is a graceful and visually delicate clumping bamboo, with a froth of small leaves hanging from the long and plentiful branches. Tall and slender in culm structure, the new culms have an intensely blue-white bloom that becomes visible when the protective papery sheaths are shed during the summer months. The old culms ripen to a pale yellow-green, providing a two-tone effect when contrasted with the new culms.

Culms: 2 cm (0.8 in.)

Leaves: 15 × 1 cm (6 × 0.4 in.). Long, narrow and willow-like

Hardiness and aspect

Min. −13°C (9°F), zone 7
Light shade

Dimensions

Height: 3–4.5 m (10–13 ft.), average 3.5 m (11.5 ft.)
Spread: 80–1.5 m (2.6–5 ft.) in 10 years

Uses and combinations

Place as a specimen amongst other established bamboos, just to add to the collection! Contrasts well with shorter, bold leaved plants that will not block the view of the naked, colourful culms. The ivy and *Fatsia* hybrid, ×*Fatshedera lizei* and the easily pruned *Mahonia aquifolium* 'Atropurpurea' are suitable candidates.

The genus *Borinda* is still controversial as it is not yet widely recognised by many botanists. The varying habits and criteria of flowering, branching patterns and rhizome systems do not exactly match the patterns and principles of some other high-altitude genera such as *Fargesia*, *Thamnocalamus* and some *Yushania*, so a new genus (*Borinda*) was formed until its various characteristics could be better assessed over time. If you try to source this plant, some suppliers will list it under *Fargesia* or *Thamnocalamus*. Such is life, always confusing!

This plant is perhaps not as widely available as many of the bamboos in this book, as it used to be

> *"The stunning pale blue culms are unsurpassed in this genus ..."*

Checklist

✓ **Non-invasive**

✗ Short (0.3–1.5 m)

✓ **Medium (1.5–3.5 m)**

✗ Tall (3.5 m +)

✓ **Cold hardy**

✗ Heat tolerant

✓ **Drought tolerant**

✗ Moisture tolerant

✓ **Pots and containers**

✓ **Good for plant association**

✓ **Waterside planting**

✓ **Hedging, screening and windbreaks**

→ New culm of *Borinda albocera*

extremely rare and of dubious hardiness. It has now been found to perform well and is only damaged during lengthy spells of a severe winter, quickly recovering the following summer from any leaf loss. Young plants often do need some support and patience, as new culms appear quite profusely at first but often rot back late in summer due to the inability of the young root and rhizome system to support the new culms. As the underground parts become more plentiful, the growth above ground becomes stronger and reaches maturity far more quickly.

As with most bamboos from this genus, they are best planted in light shade and away from winds. Its profuse branching gives it the flexibility to be lightly pruned and a carefully manicured plant should be the result. The stunning pale blue culms and dark hairy sheaths are, in my opinion, unsurpassed in this genus. These young culms eventually lose their sheen, turning a soft yellow-green in subsequent years and contrasting well with the new annual supply of blue culms.

However, this bamboo is buyer beware, as a glut of (as yet unnamed) new bamboos have recently arisen in competition with it, many with similar but perhaps slightly inferior colouring. There is also more than one clone of *Borinda albocera*, so any purchase made should always have the clone number on the label with the letter Y for the Chinese province of Yunnan where they were collected, namely Y1, Y2, Y3A and Y3B. The clone Y3A is the clone described here but Y2 is similar, with slightly larger leaves.

Look out for

Borinda edulis (Yunnan 4) has thick, glaucous culms and dark red-brown sheathing. *Borinda perlonga* (Yunnan 6) is robust and reliably hardy with arching greenery from silvery culms.

Borinda papyrifera
Papyrifera Bamboo

This is vertical and clumping with bright, steel-blue new culms, sparse branching and medium sized pale green leaves. The sheaths protecting the new culms drop quickly after colouring a rich crimson brown in good light.
Culms: 2 cm (0.8 in.)
Leaves: 14 x 2.25 cm (5 x 1 in.). Medium to long, grey-green in colour.

Hardiness and aspect

Min. −10°C (14°F), zone 8
Light shade

Dimensions

Height: 5–8 m (16–26 ft.), average 6 m (20 ft.)
Spread: 80–1.5 m (2.6–5 ft.) in 10 years

Uses and combinations

A bamboo of such beauty deserves a space of its own, but a dark solid background would highlight the conspicuous powdery culms. Low grasses and sedges such as the variegated *Carex* 'Evergold' and *Carex* 'Ice Dance' planted with low mounds of magenta *Geranium* would produce a cool but bright colour scheme.

As with *B. albocerea* there is some confusion regarding the naming this plant, as it is often listed under *Fargesia*, not to mention the two or three different clones with lengthy collectors' references. However, they are all good forms, but this description refers to my favourite – collection number CS 1064 by Chris Stapleton and the Royal Botanical Gardens, Kew.

This reliably clump forming species is one of the most robust within the genus, attaining height quickly with wider spaced culms. The new, bright blue culms are vertical and sparse in leaf at the end of the first year. Foliage becomes denser during the next two years, making the older culms arch slightly, so for a more rigid effect, many of these can be removed at the base on maturing plants without any harm to the vigour – a job best carried out during the dormant winter months to avoid damaging any newly emerging culms. A very high altitude bamboo, this *Borinda* requires cool temperate conditions and does not relish climates with high heat humidity – its foliage will become damaged and its culm growth leggy. Earlier to shoot than most within the genus, it is less prone to culm death, with new growth

*"The most
rewarding
of the recent
introductions ..."*

Checklist

✓ **Non-invasive**

✗ Short (0.3–1.5 m)

✗ Medium (1.5–3.5 m)

✓ **Tall (3.5 m +)**

✓ **Cold hardy**

✗ Heat tolerant

✓ **Drought tolerant**

✗ Moisture tolerant

✓ **Pots and containers**

✓ **Good for plant association**

✓ **Waterside planting**

✓ **Hedging, screening and windbreaks**

→ Stunning new blue culms of *Borinda papyrifera*

maturing well before the onset of cooler days. A hard winter may cause a few problems with leaf loss and branch die-back, however this bamboo's ability to recover quickly the following summer has been noted.

Now becoming more widely available, although demand still exceeds supply, so expect to pay the price. Gardeners and nurseries I have contacted regard this as the most rewarding of the recent introductions, both in speed of development and the spectacular blue culm colouring. A high accolade indeed!

Look out for

Nothing can really compare with this bamboo, but for better hardiness *Borinda (Fargesia) yulongshanensis* holds the title for the highest altitude of the Sino-Himalayan bamboos and is undeniably tough as old boots. It takes a little longer to produce a glut of silvery-blue culms but is worth the wait. The high branches on mature culms are often stained deep garnet-red and produce hanging layers of tiny leaves.

Chimonobambusa marmorea 'Variegata'
Variegated-Leaved Marbled Bamboo

A short bamboo, spreading into irregular colonies of randomly spaced culms to create miniature Japanese groves. The thin but stout culms are burnished yellow through to deep amber and appear almost red in good light. The multiple branches hold bunches of splayed leaves at the top of the culms, most of which are only slightly striped yellow-white, despite the epithet of the name.

Culms: 1 cm (0.4 in.)
Leaves: 10 × 1 cm (4 × 0.4 in.)

Hardiness and aspect
Min. −20°C (−4°F), zone 6
Sun or light shade

Dimensions
Height: 1–2.5 m (3.3–8.2 ft.), average 1.5 m (5 ft.)
Spread: 1–2.5 m (3.3–8.2 ft.) in 10 years

Uses and combinations
One of the few plants said to thrive in cool conservatories as well as in pots, as long as it is judiciously thinned on an annual basis. The culm colour is striking in the sun, so carefully prune the lower branches for a tufted effect. Great in raised or contained beds where a silver birch (or three) will look magnificent erupting through the low greenery.

An early introduction from Japan in 1889, this was a Victorian favourite when associating with *Aspidistra* and ferns in large conservatories. If planted outside in an unconfined spot, it will form a short, random grove. Although more refined than the rest of the species, this plant is still a competent invader, so unless you want to seriously annoy your neighbours, confine it to bounds.

This plant is adaptable to most soils except the very poor and dry and is also late shooting, sometimes beginning in early winter and then branching into leaf the following spring. The new culms have marbled sheathing with silvery blotches on a deep purple-brown. After the sheaths drop, the yellow culms will become visible and the burnished orange-red glow of those in full sun will impress you.

A most useful candidate for the sectional planting of a parterre, as long as the rhizomes are confined by the narrow hedges. This can be done simply with some concrete or treated timber edging at least 30 cm (1 ft.) deep. As the rhizome is shallow, it is more likely to creep over than under the barrier. Used in this fashion, the bamboo will become denser and can be clipped regularly for a more formal appearance. However, this confinement will also mean that careful removal of very old culms is necessary to avoid congestion. Plants in containers will need similar nurturing, as they do tend to yellow quickly from chlorosis. Regular splitting or potting on is required, as there is a limit to how much a starved and pot-bound plant can be fed due to residue build up from the constant addition of fertilizer. This usually changes the pH of the compost, making it more alkaline, which further induces the chlorosis or yellowing of the foliage.

Often used for path edging because of its shortness and resilience to pruning and tidying, this plant is also useful underplanting for any manner of trees and large shrubs. If you have a large natural pond, this is a fine bamboo for planting along the bank, as it will look good in the distance and have the bonus of stabilising the soil.

"Useful under-planting for any manner of trees and large shrubs"

Checklist

✗ Non-invasive

✓ **Short (0.3–1.5 m)**

✗ Medium (1.5–3.5 m)

✗ Tall (3.5 m +)

✓ **Cold hardy**

✓ **Heat tolerant**

✗ Drought tolerant

✗ Moisture tolerant

✓ **Pots and containers**

✓ **Good for plant association**

✓ **Waterside planting**

✓ **Hedging, screening and windbreaks**

→ Marbled sheathing on new culms of *Chimonobambusa marmorea* 'Variegata'

Look out for

Chimonobambusa marmorea is identical in structure to 'Variegata' but is completely green, slightly taller and usually more vigorous. *Chimonobambusa quadrangularis* is much larger in all its parts, averaging 4 m (13 ft.) in height and has a prolific, wandering habit and almost square culms. There are three more diminutive forms of the latter, all having slightly variegated striping on the leaves and golden or gold and green striped culms, namely 'Nagaminea', 'Suow' and 'Tatejima'.

← *Chimonobambusa quadrangularis* 'Suow'

Checklist

✗ Non-invasive

✗ Short (0.3–1.5 m)

✓ **Medium (1.5–3.5 m)**

✗ Tall (3.5 m +)

✓ **Cold hardy**

✓ **Heat tolerant**

✓ **Drought tolerant**

✓ **Moisture tolerant**

✓ **Pots and containers**

✓ **Good for plant association**

✓ **Waterside planting**

✗ Hedging, screening and windbreaks

← The saucer-like, swollen nodes on mature culms of *Chimonobambusa tumidissinoda*

Chimonobambusa tumidissinoda
Qiong Bamboo or Walking Stick Bamboo

A remarkable and distinct bamboo, with swollen, saucer-like nodes and weeping, layered canopies of fingered foliage. Apart from the obvious novelty value, it is a plant of great beauty.

Culms: 3 cm (1.2 in.). Rich green, softening with age
Leaves: 10 × 1 cm (4 × 0.4 in.). Long, thin and papery

Hardiness and aspect
Min. −13°C (8.5°F), zone 7
Light shade

Dimensions
Height: 3–6 m (10–20 ft.), average 3.5 m (11.5 ft.)
Spread: 3–10 m (10–33 ft.) in 10 years

Uses and combinations
Due to its wildly aggressive rhizome behaviour, this is not a plant for the timid or a small garden unless religiously contained. A large woodland setting with filtering sunlight to highlight the culms and cast delicate leaf shadows is most effective. As a feature in a pot amongst other peculiarities of the plant world, it will feel much at home and never fail to stimulate interest from visitors!

A rare Chinese native introduced to Europe in 1987, this was cherished in its locality for making walking sticks. It is unique in structural appearance on account of the very swollen saucer-like swellings on the culm nodes. The culms are rich green, toning to a pale olive-yellow and the leaves are long and narrow, hanging artistically from the high branches of mature plants.

I have seen this bamboo in numerous places, each having its own distinct habit in accordance with its location. On dry land, it favours light shade where the thin leaves can be prevented from scorching in the sun. In full sun, it prefers rich and moisture retentive soils where the water in the leaves can be replaced quickly.

Seemingly uncontained by any form of underground rhizome barrier, it is skilled at sneaking up, over and back into the soil before you even notice. This bamboo's invasive nature is not easily vanquished, and I must admit that I have sold many of these plants for use in containers to customers who cannot resist the temptation. As with any purchase, I explain the best and worst scenarios. The best is that the plant develops into a specimen of great charm and character when confined, particularly when old culms and low branches are thinned and removed frequently. The (preventable) worst case would involve the pot exploding due to the expansion of the rhizome, if it doesn't try to escape over the side of the pot first! Continual potting and/or dividing every few years will keep the plant well fed in addition to giving the rhizome room to develop. Protecting the plant in winter in a very sheltered spot or a cold glasshouse will help prevent desiccation of the foliage, something often seen on exposed bamboos in pots over the winter.

Look out for
There is now a larger-leafed form of this species, as yet with no name, which is equally vigorous but appears to be fresher in winter, particularly in containers. Buy it if you can.

Checklist

✓ **Non-invasive**

✗ Short (0.3–1.5 m)

✗ Medium (1.5–3.5 m)

✓ **Tall (3.5 m +)**

✓ **Cold hardy**

✓ **Heat tolerant**

✓ **Drought tolerant**

✗ Moisture tolerant

✗ Pots and containers

✓ **Good for plant association**

✓ **Waterside planting**

✓ **Hedging, screening and windbreaks**

← A compact form of *Chusquea culeou*

Chusquea culeou
Chilean Bamboo

Distinctive and unique, with stiff vertical culms arching only slightly at the tops. The leafy and short branching habit around the nodes on the culms has a certain individuality and flair that is reminiscent of many other southern hemisphere plants. It has a clumping habit with well spaced culms.

Culms: Maximum diameter 3 cm (1.2 in.). Deep green paling to olive yellow, while young canes are often purple tinted.

Leaves: 10 × 1 cm (4 × 0.4 in.) on average. Deep green and narrow, varying in length between clones.

Hardiness and aspect

Min. −18°C (0°F), zone 6

Sun or light woodland

Dimensions

Height: 4–7.5 m (13–24.5 ft.), average 6 m (20 ft.)

Spread: 75 cm–1.5 m (2.5–5 ft.) in 10 years

Uses and combinations

This is an imposing feature, so avoid surrounding it with other large plants. The spaced culms allow light into the clump, enabling drought tolerant ground cover to weave in and around it. The various forms of *Vinca minor* (lesser periwinkle) are surprising and effective, particularly during their late spring flowering.

A variable species both in gardens and in the wild, due to its diversity of locations. Mostly found in Chile, this bamboo is present up to the snowline of the Andes, a good indication of its hardiness and resilience against the elements. Some clones have very dark red or purple new culms that are enhanced and guaranteed when grown in full sun. For all its beauty, this *Chusquea* can be slow to mature but the reward is well worth the wait. Although clumping, a mature specimen will require at least 2 m (6.5 ft.) of room or more at the base eventually.

The culms on all *Chusquea* are solid, so hereby a tale must be told. I have always believed that for bamboos to gain height and vertical strength, they first require an adequate supporting structure below ground. I make no apology for repeating the oft-quoted maxim, "Root before shoot." Infuriatingly, young plants can take what seems like forever to transform from a juvenile nursery plant into a feast of strong, mature culms. Unbeknownst to us, this bamboo will only mature when it is good and ready. The weight of the solid culms can only be borne by a properly formed and supportive structure down below. At this time of transformation, the new culms can sprout to double the height of the previous culms.

New culms are protected by parchment-like sheathing for between twelve to eighteen months, after which these drop to reveal pale olive-green culms with distinct nodes. The multiple branches radiate around the nodes high up on mature plants, leaving the stark but beautiful culm structure free to be admired.

This *Chusquea* is rarely available for purchase as anything but a young plant. The reason for this is that the more mature the stock plant, the less it likes to be divided, on account of the solidity of the rhizome structure. Young plants may also not be suitable for propagating annually, being slow to recover and shoot, so they are rarely grown on to become larger sale plants. The appearance of a young plant can also be less than appealing, as they are quick to react to any compost deficiencies or incorrect moisture contents, with their leaves turning pale yellow-green or brown at the margins.

Look out for

Chusquea culeou 'Tenuis' is much smaller in stature, usually growing wider than it is high. Patience is again required for it to perform. There are also some named clones of the species with terrific new purple culm colourings, namely 'Purple Splendour' and 'Cana Prieta'. Both are an essential purchase if you can find them!

← *Chusquea culeou* 'Purple Splendour'

Chusquea gigantea
Giant Foxtail Bamboo

A very large Andean species, forming a large stand of well spaced vertical and thick culms holding cascading greenery from up high. Leaves quite small and plentiful. Although clumping, demands space to display its majesty.

Culms: Maximum diameter 6 cm (2.4 in.), sea green paling to olive yellow. Old culms often become yellow and red tinted.

Leaves: 12 × 1 cm (5 × 0.4 in.)

Hardiness and aspect

Min. −18°C (0°F), zone 6
Sun or light shade

Dimensions

Height: 6–16 m (20–52 ft.), average 10 m (33 ft.)
Spread: 2–5 m (6.5–16.5 ft.) in 10 years

Uses and combinations

Not for small gardens, but in large spaces use this as the dominant plant. In my opinion, a lawn surround is all you need for the best effect.

After trawling the internet for views and opinions of various bamboos, it is more than obvious that this *Chusquea* is one of the most rewarding of the temperate bamboos. I do have to concur, particularly after reading such gems as, "Creates an awe inspiring, impressive clump." One enthusiastic devotee went as far as stating that it was "the Holy Grail to many lovers of bamboos." It's more than enough to make you go out and buy one.

There have been a few name changes and misunderstandings as regards this bamboo, both in the trade and amongst botanists. This aside, make sure you see before you buy! The instantly recognisable difference between this and *Chusquea culeou* is the presence of one very long, arching primary branch surrounded by shorter ones, particularly on the upper culm nodes. This feature produces a cascade of long narrow leaves well above the impressive basal culm structure on mature specimens. This long primary branch is also evident on culms of two years old nursery plants, so you have no excuse for an incorrect purchase.

I mentioned earlier that *Chusquea culeou* was difficult to propagate, but *Chusquea gigantea* is worse. For all its impressive qualities and unbelievable speed of development, it is almost impossible to divide a mature plant successfully because of the robust interlocking rhizomes beneath the culms. As result, most plants are propagated from short, thin juvenile nursery stock in pots, though even these can sulk after handling, taking a year or two to heal before shooting again. This lengthy timescale and shortage of juvenile stock in the first place makes this bamboo both rare and expensive.

After you have succumbed to temptation, you won't have long to wait for the amazing metamorphosis. The ruby stained young shoots poke through in mid spring and wait patiently for warmer times. By mid summer, the new culms will have reached their heady heights and be slowly beginning to branch. New culms are vividly sheathed when extending upwards, so a striped effect is visible with the culms' internodes becoming visible between the sheathing. These sheaths remain on for the first year and are pushed off in the second year by the developing branches. Older culms are a pale lime-green, contrasting with the new, darker culms, but a maturing plant with dozens of new culms annually acts like a beacon and makes this bamboo the centre of attention.

*"The Holy Grail
to many lovers of
bamboo."*

Checklist

✓ **Non-invasive**

✗ Short (0.3–1.5 m)

✗ Medium (1.5–3.5 m)

✓ **Tall (3.5 m +)**

✓ **Cold hardy**

✓ **Heat tolerant**

✓ **Drought tolerant**

✗ Moisture tolerant

✗ Pots and containers

✓ **Good for plant association**

✓ **Waterside planting**

✓ **Hedging, screening and windbreaks**

→ *Chusquea gigantea* provides a bold and tropical touch

Look out for

Chusquea montana forms a much shorter colony of vertical culms at 2–3 m (6–10 ft.) with short bottle-brush branches. Also known as *Chuquea nigricans* in the United States.

← A new shoot of *Chusquea gigantea*

Fargesia angustissima
Oily Bamboo

A tiny-leafed species, very compact and tidy at the base which develops a fountain-like habit. New powdery culms are silvery-blue after their sheaths fall, while older culms will ripen to a shiny pale yellow-green.

Culms: 2 cm (0.8 in.)
Leaves: 5 × 0.5 cm (2 × 0.2 in.)

Hardiness and aspect
Min. −9°C (15°F), zone 8
Half or light shade

Dimensions
Height: 4–7 m (13–23 ft.), average 5 m (16.5 ft.)
Spread: 75 cm–1 m (2.5–3.3 ft.) in 10 years

Uses and combinations
I have found this to be most useful in mixed border planting, as it casts little shade and doesn't displace adjacent plantings too quickly. It can be planted with almost anything low, but as the bamboo is light and airy a darker combination of basal planting works well. Try *Euphorbia amygdaloides* var. *robbiae*, a form of spurge, or any of the Japanese lily turf such as *Ophiopogon japonicus* and its forms.

First cultivated in the United States and thought not to be too hardy by some in the United Kingdom. Known as a *Borinda* in some modern works, I still refer to it as a *Fargesia*, as it is known by this name in its native China and listed as such in the *Compendium of Chinese Bamboo*.

Young nursery plants are short, bushy and almost filigree in appearance, with a mass of thin, short culms and fine branches. After only two or three years, taller and colourful culms begin to punctuate this juvenile growth, which transform the plant into its adult, more upright structure. At this point the juvenile growth will start to die out naturally, after having completed its task of feeding and nurturing the root system. I sometimes bewilder the occasional customer or group by showing them a short two-year old and a maturing four- or five-year old specimen of this plant side by side. When I ask if they are both the same bamboo, the answer is almost always no. This is a simple way of teaching a potential buyer the difference between and the importance of the transition from a juvenile plant into adulthood. It also highlights an important point to remember when buying bamboos, which is that what you see isn't always what you get!

Fargesia angustissima is one of many within this genus that is essential panda fodder. It performs well in light shade or woodland areas, but I have also planted this in gardens of a more open and sunny aspect and so far so good – the fine leaves only roll inwards in self-protection on the hottest of days.

Forgetting this plant's short and green juvenile qualities, a mature plant displays an abundance of new slender culms annually, shooting early and reaching full height quickly. Young culms are stiff and vertical at first but after two years of branch production they start to arch gracefully. The culm sheaths are semi-persistent, dropping at the end of the first summer or early in the following season. The foliage is held on multiple horizontal branches, the leaves being tiny in comparison with the general stature of the bamboo. In a very hard winter, you can expect some defoliation, but don't worry as the bamboo is early into leaf the following spring. The speed of maturity of this bamboo is making it increasingly popular.

> *"The stiff, hairy culm sheaths are often flushed purple-red ..."*

Checklist

✓ **Non-invasive**

✗ Short (0.3–1.5 m)

✗ Medium (1.5–3.5 m)

✓ **Tall (3.5 m +)**

✓ **Cold hardy**

✓ **Heat tolerant**

✓ **Drought tolerant**

✗ Moisture tolerant

✓ **Pots and containers**

✓ **Good for plant association**

✓ **Waterside planting**

✓ **Hedging, screening and windbreaks**

→ A six-year-old plant of *Fargesia angustissima*

Look out for

Borinda fungosa and *Borinda perlonga*, although both could turn into *Fargesia* when the botanists have finished deliberating. They are both similar in habit with larger leaves and much thicker culms. Young plants may be damaged in the first few winters, but the older they get the stronger they become.

"Certainly one of the best bamboos for cool regions."

Checklist

✓ **Non-invasive**

✗ Short (0.3–1.5 m)

✗ Medium (1.5–3.5 m)

✓ **Tall (3.5 m +)**

✓ **Cold hardy**

✓ **Heat tolerant**

✓ **Drought tolerant**

✗ Moisture tolerant

✓ **Pots and containers**

✓ **Good for plant association**

✓ **Waterside planting**

✓ **Hedging, screening and windbreaks**

← Two or three plants of *Fargesia denudata* planted closely will form an effective screen

Fargesia denudata
Giant Panda Fodder Bamboo

A beautiful clumping bamboo with an abundance of thin but strong, whippy culms turning quickly from green to orange-yellow, especially in full sun. Small, blunt, fresh green leaves are broad for their size and through their weight help to produce a distinct arching profile with age.

Culms: 1.5 cm (0.6 in.)
Leaves: 5 × 1.5 cm (2 × 0.6 in.)

Hardiness and aspect

Min. −23°C (−10°F), zone 6
Sun or half shade

Dimensions

Height: 3–5 m (10–16.5 ft.), average 4 m (13 ft.)
Spread: 75 cm–1 m (2.5–3.3 ft.) in 10 years

Uses and combinations

Seems to last for ages in large containers without much attention except the necessary watering. A dark, distant background will help to focus attention on the compact, bole-like display of the culms. Splash a few dark evergreen ferns nearby as simple companions, as these are mostly drought tolerant, useful because the bamboo will take the water first.

Although there are different forms of this species now in cultivation, this description relates to the clone introduced by Roy Lancaster, namely his collection L1575. This is certainly one of the best bamboos for cool regions, being extremely hardy and winter tolerant, suffering little or no damage.

Once again, young nursery plants do not do the finished product any justice, as they are usually lax in habit and sparse in leaf. Young plants also seem to shoot later than established ones and often do not fully branch and leaf in the first season. Beyond this frustration, the plant will quickly become more plentiful, much stronger and start to show its true

colours within four or five years. I have a specimen that has lived in a large tub for at least eight years and it looks almost as good now as it did when potted up. Unbelievably, the bamboo has not been fed in this time (apart from the initial dose of slow release fertilizer lasting one year), just watered when it needed it. The starvation has paled the leaves very slightly but has helped colour many of the older culms a glossy mustard-yellow.

When planted in the open ground, this bamboo will be lush and mainly green for many years, the older culms eventually turning brighter with age. The new, pale culm sheaths remain for the first year and contrast well with the rest of the plant. The short but plentiful branches mean that old culms that arch too much with the weight of the foliage can be lightly shortened – this weight release makes the plant more vertical. Old culms have a long life expectancy and little or no thinning is required.

Look out for

Fargesia denudata Xian 1 and Xian 2 are two good clones that differ only in the smallest detail. If you can't find the described L1575, then these are almost as good.

Fargesia murielae
Umbrella Bamboo

Pale green with arching culms that gradually turn yellow-green. A mass of small, pale greenery will tumble from the tight clump of a mature plant. This species and its cultivars are simply identified by having an overall softer green colouring than the rest of the genus.
Culms: 1.5 cm (0.6 in.)
Leaves: 8 × 1 cm (3 × 0.4 in.)

Hardiness and aspect

Min. −29°C (−20°F), zone 5
Sun or light shade.

Dimensions

Height: 3–4.5 m (10–14.8 ft.), average 4 m (13 ft.)
Spread: 75 cm–1.2 m (2.5–4 ft.) in 10 years

"Layers of fresh green foliage move with the slightest breeze."

Checklist
✓ **Non-invasive**
✗ Short (0.3–1.5 m)
✗ Medium (1.5–3.5 m)
✓ **Tall (3.5 m +)**
✓ **Cold hardy**
✓ **Heat tolerant**
✓ **Drought tolerant**
✗ Moisture tolerant
✓ **Pots and containers**
✓ **Good for plant association**
✓ **Waterside planting**
✓ **Hedging, screening and windbreaks**

← A mature specimen of *Fargesia murielae*

Uses and combinations

This species and its cultivars form the tightest of clumps, are tidy and need little or no maintenance, ideal for those who like neatness and order. I have seen this species erupt proudly from herbaceous borders, in colourful winter gardens with dogwoods and willows and also in solitude amongst shady woodland plantings where the freshness of the foliage illuminates the gloom.

This plant is one of the reasons for the popularity of bamboos worldwide, as it is unquestionably hardy. It was introduced into the United States in 1907 and then Europe in 1913. After a flowering phase during the late 1970s there is now a multitude of different clones and cultivars.

The culms are abundant and slender, emerging blue-green from between the sheaths and ripening to a pale yellow-green during the course of the following two or three seasons. As the branches and foliage develop to their full complement in the year

→ A fresh young nursery plant of *Fargesia murielae* 'Simba' in the summer.

after shooting, the culms begin to arch gracefully. Layers of fresh green foliage move with the slightest breeze, flickering enticingly in the shadows of dappled shade. Although all *Fargesia* species lose some old leaves before the onset of winter, this bamboo makes it more obvious, as its old leaves turn a pale buttery colour before dropping two or three weeks later. Aside from this brief and necessary lightening of the load to prevent excess desiccation, the species is the freshest of plants in a garden. However, in pots, I would select the cultivars that perform better when restricted.

Look out for

There are three outstanding cultivars with similar pale leaf colouring to the species but with different habits. *Fargesia murielae* 'Bimbo' is, as the name suggests, short and cute with small leaves, growing no more than 2 m (6.5 ft.) high. 'Simba' (pictured) is more popular and well known, as it was one of the first distinct seedlings to be propagated widely. This specimen has paler foliage and is extremely compact, reaching a maximum of 2.5 m (8.2 ft.). 'Jumbo' has broader leaves than the species and appears to be more vigorous, growing slightly taller. All are good in pots.

Fargesia nitida
Fountain Bamboo

This plant has slender, arching culms which are deep green at first but then become dark purple with age. New culms are attractively sheathed during the first growing season and (apart from a leaf or two at the tips) remain devoid of branches, which develop in the second year with narrow, grey-green leaves. Mature plants have a distinct habit akin to a mushroom cloud.

Culms: 1.5 cm (0.6 in.)
Leaves: 5 × 1.5 cm (2 × 0.6 in.)

Hardiness and aspect

Min. −29°C (−20°F), zone 5
Light or half shade

Dimensions

Height: 3–4 m (10–13 ft.), average 3 m (10 ft.)
Spread: 60 cm–1 m (2–3.3 ft.) in 10 years

Uses and combinations

Extremely versatile and is capable of good performance in quite deep shade. Good for tidy hedging, lawn specimens, waterside planting and mixed borders. A basal planting of larger leaved bamboos such as *Indocalamus tessellatus* and *Sasa veitchii* will clearly define these opposites within the bamboo group.

The delicate appearance of this bamboo belies its hardiness and as a result it has been widely planted for its beauty. Unfortunately, as explained in the section on flowering, all mature plants, forms and cultivars of the species have flowered and died. Yet all is not lost, as the glut of seed produced as a result means that the next generation of young plants are already in cultivation and much in demand. Many gardeners who have lost this plant through flowering would normally be put off bamboos as a result, however the opposite has happened in this case. The phenomenon of death by flowering has stirred customers' interest and the desire to replace their loss with the same plant, a sure sign that this species was well favoured.

In my garden, this was my first bamboo. It was a young slip of a plant that looked lost amongst the grasses and woody shrubs I had planted when the garden was in its infancy some twenty-five years ago. It sulked for a year or two and then to my surprise, suddenly catapulted a myriad of new leafless culms skyward. As I was a novice at the time, I understood little about this but was compelled to find out more about this plant. After another year in the ground and seeing the transition of the naked culms into branches and leaves, I rapidly became addicted to the wonderful group of bamboos. My original plant was the true species, but I eventually purchased or was given other forms and cultivars. Sadly, all these have now died after passing through the cycle of flowering, but thanks to their regeneration (and possible hybridization) there is already a new selection of seedling clones on the way. These are still young, so it is difficult to be precise regarding their final habit and structure with no mature specimens available to judge.

The first batch of seedlings I produced here on the nursery is showing dark new culms after only three years, similar to those of the original species. When my specimen of *Fargesia nitida* was in all its glory in the garden, it never failed to impress. Although the culms were crowded, with little or no space between them, they were naturally bare at the base with the high branches of pointed grey-green leaves cascading elegantly outwards. The greyness of the foliage and the dark, almost purple-black culm colouring with the paler sheathing was the best advertisement I ever had for encouraging customers to make a purchase.

In my early days of bamboo hunting when I was trying to expand my stock, I often came across this plant labelled as the 'Black Bamboo' which is correctly *Phyllostachys nigra*. In fact, to this day I still receive telephone calls and customers here who insist on telling me that their 'Black Bamboo' has just flowered, but the description given is always that of *Fargesia nitida*.

Look out for

As described previously, there is likely to be a plentiful supply of new clones available due to flowering. My prized specimen of *Fargesia nitda* 'Nymphenburg' has been the last of the forms to flower in my garden, but I now have seedlings as a result. I only hope they retain the same habit as their parent, which was taller than the species with grey-blue, thicker culms and the most delicate of leaves. It had a unique habit and in the rain I could shelter under the overhanging branches.

Fargesia nitida 'Jiuzhaigou' has numerous forms, but clones one, two and four are the pick of the crop. These were collected as early seedlings during the mid 1980s in Jiuzhaigou National Park in China at a high altitude. 'Jiuzhaigou One' has already earned the name of 'Red Fountain Bamboo', the older culms developing a deep crimson-red colouring in good light. 'Jiuzhaigou Two' is shorter, with similar dark colouring, taking longer to develop but has tiny leaves. 'Jiuzhaigou Four' has stunning deep purple-black culms even on young plants. I have not seen a good size plant of the latter as it is new to me, but the colouration is promising alone.

"In all its glory in the garden, it never failed to impress."

Checklist

✓ Non-invasive

✗ Short (0.3–1.5 m)

✓ Medium (1.5–3.5 m)

✗ Tall (3.5 m +)

✓ Cold hardy

✓ Heat tolerant

✓ Drought tolerant

✗ Moisture tolerant

✓ Pots and containers

✓ Good for plant association

✓ Waterside planting

✓ Hedging, screening and windbreaks

→ The tightly packed culms of *Fargesia nitida* holding the greenery aloft

→ *Fargesia nitida* 'Nymphenburg'

"Some exciting quirks and charms to keep you entertained."

Checklist
- ✓ **Non-invasive**
- ✗ Short (0.3–1.5 m)
- ✗ Medium (1.5–3.5 m)
- ✓ **Tall (3.5 m +)**
- ✓ **Cold hardy**
- ✓ **Heat tolerant**
- ✓ **Drought tolerant**
- ✗ Moisture tolerant
- ✓ **Pots and containers**
- ✓ **Good for plant association**
- ✓ **Waterside planting**
- ✓ **Hedging, screening and windbreaks**

← A young specimen of *Fargesia robusta*, still to mature

← The pale sheathing of *Fargesia robusta* starting to drop from the culms in mid-summer

Fargesia robusta
Robusta Bamboo

Dark, glossy green new culms are vividly sheathed, appearing almost pure white at the height of summer, then falling to show their rich, lustrous colouring against the paler old culms. Shiny tapering leaves are held high and point downwards at 45 degrees. Young plants may arch slightly but mature specimens are staunchly vertical with just a flick of outward branching at the top.

Culms: 2.5 cm (1 in.)
Leaves: 13 × 2 cm (5 × 0.75 in.)

Hardiness and aspect

Min. −18°C (0°F), zone 6
Sun or light shade

Dimensions

Height: 4–6 m (13–20 ft.), average 5 m (16.5 ft.)
Spread: 75 cm–1.5 m (2.5–5 ft.) in 10 years

Uses and combinations

I have seen this bamboo far and wide in many different situations and aspects. It is at home in pots, narrow raised beds, light woodland areas, exposed locations and also as screens, boundaries and hedging. My plant is in the shade of a very large Scots pine and it lights up the dimness with its ebullient display of summer sheathing. In the foreground I have the red flowered *Persicaria amplexicaulis* 'Atrosanguinea' and *Ribes sanguineum* 'Brocklebankii', the red and the pale gold also piercing the gloom.

Outstanding is the best description of this bamboo in this useful genus. But to allay any possible confusion, if this species is seen with the epithet – Campbell, then it is likely to be the true species, referring to the first of the introductions to the West. Although a recent introduction, this species has already proved its garden worthiness widely in the West.

The early new shoots appear as dark, sharp points in the chill of March and with the first of the warmer days they emerge slowly to flaunt their bristly armour of crimson and lime green sheathing a few inches above the ground. In the warmth, they expand upwards losing this early colouration and by midsummer will have reached their full height, the branches and leaves following shortly. The culm internodes become a deep emerald-green and are highlighted with the ghostly, alternating white sheathing in a beacon-like display. The sheaths gradually turn parchment coloured, hinging and falling from the tops of the culms downwards in unison. As autumn and winter approach, the gloss of the culms and leaves becomes more vivid – they positively glow with health in the flickering shafts of sunlight. In good light, a faint tinge of crimson develops on the branch points, lasting well into the following season.

It is easy to sing the praises of this species, which I frequently do to entice a customer. It is early to shoot, which means it is plentiful and quick to mature. It is versatile, tidy, requires virtually no maintenance and, indeed, lives up to its specific name of *robusta*. When I say that is in the top five of my bamboos (along with the other ten or twenty), the customer is already smitten. By the way, did I mention its tolerance of drought? The fleshy roots act as additional storage organs to the rhizomes.

One of the best specimens I have seen was growing in solitude in a raised bed. The bed was long and narrow and the bamboo had been naturally forced sideways and was growing right up to the retaining brickwork. Clusters of old culms had been carefully thinned out to leave individual colonies appearing almost like separate plants. This bamboo was regularly watered in times of summer and winter drought and also had a high nitrogen liquid feed applied sparingly to it during the warmer growing season. In contrast, the plant in my garden has never been touched – it is difficult to force a hand between the densely packed culms, as no light from behind appears through them.

Look out for

There are three good forms of the species. 'Pingwu', should you prefer something shorter and arching, is relatively new. It is scruffy at first but becomes better

← Red branch bracts on *Fargesia robusta* 'Red Sheath'

groomed with age. 'Red Sheath' is my favourite, with a flare of persistent deep coppery-red sheathing at the base of each branch. This plant also has slightly broader leaves. 'Wolong' has even larger leaves, at two or three times the size of the species, occasional red colouring and is more vigorous and open in culm habit. All carry the same pale summer sheathing like the species.

Fargesia rufa
Gansu 95–1

The shortest plant in the genus, forming a plant wider than it is high, although this plant reaches maturity relatively quickly. The earliest bamboo to shoot in western gardens, this bamboo has conspicuous pale red sheathing on the culms and branches. A plentiful complement of matte sea green leaves adorn the congested branches. Culms are slender and arch majestically outwards on mature plants, touching the ground with their tips and hiding the culms at the base.

Culms: 1 cm (0.4 in.)
Leaves: 8 × 0.75 cm (3 × 0.3 in.)

Hardiness and aspect

Min. −20°C (−4°F), zone 6
Sun or light shade

Dimensions

Height: 2–3.5 m (6.5–11.5 ft.), average 2.5 m (8.2 ft.)

Spread: 75 cm–1.5 m (2.5–4 ft.) in 10 years

Uses and combinations

Perfect for pots where it will reach and remain at 2 m (6.5 ft.). Good for clipping due to the dense branch structure as the cuts are quickly covered over by new growth. Plant in drifts in woodland clearings, along the edges of a driveway or in a mixed border for some winter structure. Also offers an alternative to larger leaved bamboos such as *Pseudosasa japonica*.

A very recent introduction from the 1990s, this bamboo is already a hugely popular selection, as it is ideal for the ever fashionable theme of container gardening. Although some of this genus occasionally show stress when grown in pots by rolling their leaves inwards during extreme heat, cold or wind, *Fargesia rufa* rarely does.

In my garden, this bamboo is in the most inhospitable place, which is shady and bone-dry

"Early shooting means it generates a prolific quantity of culms."

Checklist

✓ **Non-invasive**

✗ Short (0.3–1.5 m)

✓ **Medium (1.5–3.5 m)**

✗ Tall (3.5 m +)

✓ **Cold hardy**

✓ **Heat tolerant**

✓ **Drought tolerant**

✗ Moisture tolerant

✓ **Pots and containers**

✓ **Good for plant association**

✓ **Waterside planting**

✓ **Hedging, screening and windbreaks**

→ Even in early February, this *Fargesia* shows no sign of winter damage

in summer, because the water is first used by the surrounding mature trees. In winter, it is exposed on all sides as the bare trunks of the trees offer no shelter – this plant takes the full blow of the wind from all directions in its stride. This area is also often flooded in the winter, being low lying. Yet for all its misplacement, *Fargesia rufa* shows much satisfaction in defiance of its aspect.

After planting a young propagule with a few spindly culms some six or seven years ago, I now have a specimen whose foliage canopy arches outwards as wide as the plant is high, at 2.5 m (8.2 ft.). Yet underneath the skirt of layered foliage, the width of the culm base is just less than 1 m (3.3 ft.). The early new shoots punch through the foliage canopy by late spring, with coppery sheathing above each of the nodes. This persists for most of the first season but the similarly coloured sheathing on the opening branches remains on much longer, offering a rich tone within the sea-green foliage.

The previous year's shoots increase their combined leaf weight and gradually arch outwards, creating another layer to the parachute of foliage. The length between the upper internodes on the culms is quite short and it also has many branches that point outwards at acute angles. When pruning, weight is released from each culm, allowing them to spring back upwards, revealing the structure below.

This bamboo's early shooting means it generates a prolific quantity of culms annually, making it quick to mature. A young plant supplied with five or six short culms will easily have at least ten times this number within three years. Its ability to regenerate quickly from heavy thinning and hard pruning is also a likely reason as to why it one of the feeding plants of the giant panda.

← The unusual leaf shape of *Fargesia dracocephala*

Look out for

Fargesia rufa – variegated. As yet with no other name, this plant is virtually identical to the species, except for a creamy flush on the terminal branches during mid to late summer. This colouring appears more readily in full sun and especially on older plants when slightly stressed. Young nursery plants are shy to colour at all. *Fargesia dracocephala* is another shortish offering, growing 2–3 m (6.5–10 ft.) in height with a unique leaf arrangement, with its green leaves tapering to fine points at both ends. Not good in pots as it stresses too easily, but in the ground it is always of rich appearance.

Fargesia scabrida
Scabrida Bamboo

Instantly recognizable with slim but strong dusky culms and vivid red sheathing. The narrow, hanging leaves are very dark compared to others in the genus. Clumping with a more upright habit than most when mature, arching only slightly at the tips.

Culms: Maximum 6 mm (0.25 in.)
Leaves: 7 × 1.25 cm (2.75 × 0.5 in.)

Hardiness and aspect

Min. −18°c (0°F), zone 6
Sun or part shade

Dimensions

Height: 3.5–5 m (11.5–16.5 ft.), average 4 m (13 ft.)
Spread: 1–1.5 m (3.3 –5 ft.) in 10 years

Uses and combinations

Such darkness in a bamboo is unusual but welcome. As it is a vigorous clumper, try brightening around the base with easily moveable plants such as ornamental grasses and perennials. Low evergreen sedges such as the bronze *Carex flagellifera* and the dark, russet leaved *Bergenia* are similar in hue to the *Fargesia*, so add swathes *Luzula sylvatica* 'Aurea' with its winter brightness, or the self seeding *Milium effusum* 'Aureum'.

At this moment in time, there are no really mature plants of this species to assess, as it was not available in Europe until the late 1990s. Heights and dimensions given here are based on their description in the *Chinese Compendium of Bamboos*. This useful tome

"This fine bamboo is already proving most useful with its versatility."

Checklist

✓ **Non-invasive**

✗ Short (0.3–1.5 m)

✗ Medium (1.5–3.5 m)

✓ **Tall (3.5 m +)**

✓ **Cold hardy**

✓ **Heat tolerant**

✓ **Drought tolerant**

✗ Moisture tolerant

✓ **Pots and containers**

✓ **Good for plant association**

✓ **Waterside planting**

✓ **Hedging, screening and windbreaks**

→ A close-up of a new dark culm with colourful sheathing on *Fargesia scabrida*

also lists it as a clumping or pseudo-running bamboo. Having never been presented with the term pseudo-running before, I take this to mean a vigorous clump former, which it does appear to be. A young plant will stay tight, but as maturity is reached the glut of new culms that appear annually can expand the girth at the base quite quickly.

The ruby-red buds peeping through the ground sprout forth their slender dark culms at great speed, soon showing the vivid sheath colouring of deep orange-red surrounding the dark purple-green bloomy culms. The narrow, glossy leaves taper to slender points and are quite rough in texture, proof of their underlying hardiness.

This fine bamboo is already proving most useful with its versatility. Tolerant of sun, shade, and exposure, it also has a general ability to cope with the stress of prolonged frost and icy winds. A fine choice for pots or a narrow, contained border. Highly suited to the climate of the United Kingdom and mainly cool coastal locations in the United States – in inland and continental locations with high heat humidity, it would benefit from dappled shade.

I have seen this bamboo displayed at garden centres with the cultivar name 'Asian Wonder', which admittedly is a good choice of name. However, I can assure you that this is identical to the true species and that the name 'Asian Wonder' is merely a trademark given to it by the producer. Being a bit of a purist as far as plant names are concerned, it is a shame that fancy cultivar names have to be bandied about freely just to act as a tempter for purchase. It is not really necessary with this bamboo, as its appearance and garden worthiness speaks for itself.

Look out for

Fargesia ferax, sometimes listed as a *Borinda*. Still very rare and much slower to grow than *Fargesia scabrida*, its distinct lanceolate leaves on tall and slender culms show much character. Culms are pale grey-green, bloomy at first, ripening to a shiny yellow-green.

Fargesia utilis
Tung Chuan 3

Delicate branches of cascading greenery form the shape of a mushroom cloud. The enormous crown is supported by the tightest of clumps at the base, although because the foliage can arc right down to the ground, the base clump may not be visible.
Culms: Maximum 2.5 cm (1 in.). Darkens to pale green with age and very dark red in sun on young plants that have been thinned.
Leaves: 9 × 1.5 cm (4 × 0.6 in.)

Hardiness and aspect
Min. −18°C (0°F), zone 6
Sun or light shade

Dimensions
Height: 4–6 m (13–20 ft.), average 4.5 m (14.8 ft.)
Spread: 75 cm–1.2 m (2.5–4 ft.) in 10 years

Uses and combinations
Prefers absolute solitary confinement in a large border or open woodland because of its large overhang. If used for hedging, plant widely apart and have patience. The arch of the foliage from the individual plants will eventually meld to form an impenetrable barrier. As a specimen, it is a wonderful choice for lake or riverside planting to replace the ubiquitous weeping willow.

A very beautiful bamboo from the mountains of China, it can mature to be one of the tallest of the genus. Its elegant fountain-like habit does need more room than most, as the width of the foliage canopy can be five or six times that of the supporting culm structure. As you may have surmised by now, this is not a bamboo for the smallest of gardens, but if you are lucky enough to have room, this is more than essential.

When growing these plants in pots for exhibitions, I have found that the confinement often colours the upper parts of the culms and the higher branches a rich plum-red. This is not as evident on plants in the ground unless they are mature and in full light. Small, delicate leaves on the multiple branches are produced from the relatively thick culms. The culms mature

"If you are lucky enough to have room, this is more than essential."

Checklist

✓ **Non-invasive**

✗ Short (0.3–1.5 m)

✗ Medium (1.5–3.5 m)

✓ **Tall (3.5 m +)**

✓ **Cold hardy**

✓ **Heat tolerant**

✓ **Drought tolerant**

✗ Moisture tolerant

✓ **Pots and containers**

✓ **Good for plant association**

✓ **Waterside planting**

✓ **Hedging, screening and windbreaks**

→ Elegant *Fargesia utilis* (background) with *Sasa kurilensis* – short (in front)

upwards quickly and are a pale dusty-green, with protective sheathing only in the first season, except at the base where it can persist for a year or two more. Light shade is this plant's preferred aspect, as in full sun the leaves can roll for protection, similar to those of *Fargesia nitida*, with which *Fargesia utilis* is often confused as a young plant.

Large plants in containers last well even when under stress. When manicured carefully with regular thinning of older culms and light pruning, the finished effect is airy and graceful. In the open soil, apart from requiring the solitude of an open aspect, distant planting will allow for the best viewing of this bamboo's beauty and form.

Look out for

Thamnocalamus spathiflorus and its subspecies *nepalensis*. Although a different genus, these can attain a similar weeping habit. With larger, fresher and paler leaves than most *Fargesia*, they are also more open in habit, with fewer but thicker culms. These are useful bamboos for lighting up the darkest background.

Place them against a large wall where their greenery and curves will soften the hard material.

×*Hibanobambusa tranquillans* 'Shiroshima'
Shiroshima Bamboo

Although variable in habit, the bold, quite large variegated leaves on this bamboo never fail to impress. Green culms hold stiff branches with sprays of broad and long pointed leaves of a dark shining green with variable white striping on the upper surface. These can often appear mostly white and show pink-purple tinges at the height of summer.
Culms: 2 cm (0.8 in.)
Leaves: Large and pointed

Hardiness and aspect

Min. −22°C (−7°F), zone 6
Sun or half shade

Dimensions

Height: 2.5–5 m (8.2–16.5 ft.), average 3.5 m (11.5 ft.)
Spread: 75 cm–1.5 m (2.5–5 ft.) in 10 years

Uses and combinations

One of the most useful bamboos by the very nature of its colouring. Variegation can be used with almost any other colours. Blue *Geranium*, red dogwoods, purple *Cotinus* or golden prostrate junipers are simple suggestions. A dark ivy at the base such as *Hedera helix* 'Fluffy Ruffles' is equally impressive. Its association with other bamboos is spectacular – in the foreground of a dark *Phyllostachys*, its boldness and command of space is indomitable. In pots, it is easily maintained and long-lived – try pale blue ceramic or an eye-catching scarlet red for an assertive statement.

A unique bi-generic hybrid from a *Phyllostachys* and a *Sasa*, the two parents remarkably flowered at the same time by Mount Hiba in Japan. It has the larger leaves of the *Sasa* and the strong timber-like culm structure of the *Phyllostachys*.

Predicting the ultimate habit of height and spread of this bamboo is almost impossible. The plant in my garden is taller than average and, even after twenty years, has remained in a tight clump. The soil is hard clay at the bottom of a small slope which has a water run-off available to it most of the time. In a friend's garden in the neighbouring county, there are two separate plants of this hybrid. One is in a gravel border and is so tight at the base that the culm structure is impenetrable. The other was planted through permeable matting with a heavy bark mulch. Although moist at the roots, the rhizome travelled many metres in all directions. The simple moral of this story is do not plant your bamboos through any sort of soil membrane. Even though the new shoots are quite sharp and able to pierce the covering, they usually take the easy option of extending beneath it to find an easier means of escape. Although most bamboo books list this as invasive, the vast majority of plants seen on my travels have been tidy and tight.

The new shoots are artistically decorated with white and green sheathing, having small purple blades at the top of the sheaths. The culms emerge light green and quickly form pairs of branches bowing downwards as the beautifully marked, often pink tinged leaves unfold.

> "One of the most beautiful of all variegated woody plants."

Checklist

- ✗ Non-invasive
- ✗ Short (0.3–1.5 m)
- ✓ Medium (1.5–3.5 m)
- ✗ Tall (3.5 m +)
- ✓ Cold hardy
- ✓ Heat tolerant
- ✓ Drought tolerant
- ✗ Moisture tolerant
- ✓ Pots and containers
- ✓ Good for plant association
- ✓ Waterside planting
- ✓ Hedging, screening and windbreaks

→ ×*Hibanobambusa tranquillans* 'Shiroshima' with culms of *Phyllostachys vivax* f. *aureocaulis*

This bamboo can also be shaped and thinned at leisure because secondary branching occurs, providing new fresh leaves annually. On a final note, the brightness of the leaves is rarely diminished when the plant is grown in shade.

Look out for

The all green form, ×*Hibanobambusa tranquillans*, is for the purists among you who baulk at anything variegated. Slightly more vigorous and taller than its variegated partner, it is a suitable alternative to the wandering *Sasa* genus.

→ Large fresh leaves of ×*Hibanobambusa tranquillans* in winter

"For a large-leaved plant it shows great tolerance of stress."

Checklist

✗ Non-invasive

✗ Short (0.3–1.5 m)

✓ Medium (1.5–3.5 m)

✗ Tall (3.5 m +)

✓ Cold hardy

✓ Heat tolerant

✓ Drought tolerant

✗ Moisture tolerant

✓ Pots and containers

✓ Good for plant association

✓ Waterside planting

✓ Hedging, screening and windbreaks

← A group of *Indocalamus latifolius* nursery plants

← The huge leaves of *Indocalamus hamadae*

Indocalamus latifolius
Chinese Reed Bamboo

Slender and upright with deep green, very large and broad leaves held horizontally from the culms. Quite tidy in winter considering the leaf size, with minimal bleaching compared to the genus *Sasa*. Its reddish new shoots come up earlier than most, are tight and tidy for a few years then are apt to wander.

Culms: 1 cm (0.4 in.)
Leaves: 30 × 5 cm (12 × 2 in.)

Hardiness and aspect
Min. −20°C (−4°F), zone 6
Light shade

Dimensions
Height: 1.5–3 m (5–10 ft.), average 2 m (6.2 ft.)
Spread: 75 cm–1.5 m (2.5–5 ft.) in 10 years

Uses and combinations
This bamboo is just the right height for screening eyesores that are close to houses, such as rubbish bins, oil tanks, water butts and the like. Great for partitions, this plant is also a useful addition to a border or exotic planting scheme and is easily managed in pots. Impress your friends by serving them sushi on freshly cut leaves.

A useful architectural bamboo on account of its lush, tropical appearance, this plant is happy in sun or part shade. The slender culms develop early from deep red shoots and are quite straight, considering the weight of the developing leaves above. The long, broad leaves unfurl from a tight pointed roll to display their rich green lustre during early summer. The more mature the plant, the larger the leaves.

More likely to wander in dry soil – if this is the case, they do so in long straight lines and are nearly always shallow, making removal a simple task as they can be pulled out by hand. It is worth making the point here that as a general rule, any invading rhizome left in the soil for more than a year or two is much more difficult to remove because of the increased amount of feeding root that will have gripped the soil. When you see offending shoots, expose the rhizome and pull it all the way back to the mother plant and remove. Dormant buds should then become active closer to the clump and so with determination a strong tight clump can be created. In general, this bamboo is more refined in habit in cooler gardens.

I love this in pots as, strangely for a large-leaved bamboo, it shows great tolerance of stress – even if checked by slight drying out, starvation or harsh winds, it is quick to recover. Leaves that do become bleached or shredded (usually in pots) after a hard winter can easily be removed when the new ones emerge. A few minutes' work on an annual basis makes a big difference in this respect. The single, strong branching along the culms has the capability of regenerating fresh new leaves quickly to create a perfectly proportioned plant in balance with the root system that supports it.

Look out for
Indocalamus hamadae has the largest leaves of any temperate bamboo. This plant has a slightly more lax habit and more chance of winter damage, but in a sheltered place with half shade, it is well worth the challenge. Take some time to give it some annual tidying and as it matures, the extra large leaves will reach 60 cm (2 ft.) long.

"Choose this bamboo for its unique habit and tidy appearance."

Checklist

✗ Non-invasive

✓ **Short (0.3–1.5 m)**

✗ Medium (1.5–3.5 m)

✗ Tall (3.5 m +)

✓ **Cold hardy**

✓ **Heat tolerant**

✓ **Drought tolerant**

✓ **Moisture tolerant**

✓ **Pots and containers**

✓ **Good for plant association**

✓ **Waterside planting**

✓ **Hedging, screening and windbreaks**

← The large leaves and low habit of a potted *Indocalamus tessellatus*

Indocalamus tessellatus
Tessellatus

A small species that at maturity will have no visible culm structure due to the mass of the large, pointed and lush green leaves. Forms a low, leafy exotic cover and gives its best effect in cool gardens.

Culms: Maximum diameter 0.6 cm (0.25 in.), thin and matt green with thin brown sheaths.

Leaves: 45 × 8 cm (18 × 3 in.)

Hardiness and aspect

Min. −25°C (−13°F), zone 5
Sun or shade

Dimensions

Height: 1–3 m (3.3–10 ft.), average 1.5 m (5 ft.)
Spread: 75 cm–1.5 m (2.5–5 ft.) in 10 years

Uses and combinations

A splendid small plant and weed suppressant. Try it at the base of timber bamboos with a high branch system or with a colourful *Phormium* (New Zealand flax) or a *Yucca*. Resilient in pots and one of the few bamboos suited for cool, shady conservatories.

One of the earliest bamboos to be introduced to the West in 1845, it is as popular now as it was then. Even though it is short in habit, this bamboo carries the largest of leaves in comparison to its structure. The beautifully veined and slightly twisted leaves point to the ground and arch the slender culms into a mop-like feature. Short and slender culms amazingly manage to poke through the canopy of leaves, vying for their position in the light and creating another layer to the dense canopy. At this point, some thinning and removal of older growth can be done, particularly if there has been any leaf damage during the previous dormant season. As the leaves enlarge, the prominent creamy central veins become visible as the leaf tissue hardens. Further shallow ridges and troughs appear longitudinally on either side of the central vein and beautifully angle and reflect the light cast upon them.

Considering this is normally classed as invasive, I have yet to see one run riot. It does form a slowly expanding colony, but does not have the ability of some species of *Sasa* to appear suddenly in a neighbouring garden from an unseen and lengthy rhizome. In any case, as with the previous *Indocalamus latifolius*, it is easy to keep in check with a little bit of annual maintenance. I am often asked by customers for short bamboos, so I show them the full selection, but the majority choose this bamboo for its unique habit and clean and tidy appearance in pots. There really is no other small woody plant that comes close to providing such an impressive architectural presence.

Look out for

Indocalamus solidus is more invasive and has a stout, upright structure, growing to halfway between the heights of *tessellatus* and *latifolius*. The pronounced winter bleaching is attractive, making this bamboo well suited for woodland cover and stabilising slope and banks.

Indocalamus longiauritus is little known but worth the search. Slightly taller than *tessellatus*, it also has narrower and more pointed leaves.

Phyllostachys arcana 'Luteosulcata'
Yellow Grooved Arcana Bamboo

This bamboo is variable in height and spread according to placement but always stocky in appearance. It grows tidy, open groves of glossy green jointed culms with bright yellow grooves (sulci). Its leaves are shiny on the upper surface and matte grey-green below.

Culms: Maximum diameter 4 cm (1.6 in.)
Leaves: 15 × 2 cm (6 × 0.75 in.)

Hardiness and aspect

Min. −20°C (−4°F), zone 6
Sun or light shade

Checklist

- ✗ Non-invasive
- ✗ Short (0.3–1.5 m)
- ✗ Medium (1.5–3.5 m)
- ✓ **Tall (3.5 m+)**
- ✓ **Cold hardy**
- ✓ **Heat tolerant**
- ✓ **Drought tolerant**
- ✗ Moisture tolerant
- ✓ **Pots and containers**
- ✓ **Good for plant association**
- ✓ **Waterside planting**
- ✓ **Hedging, screening and windbreaks**

← The broad golden sulcus on a culm of *Phyllostachys arcana* 'Luteosulcata'

Dimensions

Height: 4–8 m (13–26 ft.), average 5 m (16.5 ft.)
Spread: 1–2.5 m (3.3–8.2 ft.) in 10 years

Uses and combinations

Strong and abundant culm production so old ones can be removed for use as garden canes. The golden striping and general gloss of the plant is effective in half shade and the open and regimented culm structure allows for woodlanders to be planted below.

My plant rarely sees the sun, being in the shade of a large Scots pine, but it is nicely vertical and tidy. Below it I have *Mahonia aquifolium* 'Repens', *Brunnera macrophylla* 'Langtrees' and *Symphytum* (comfrey), all simple but effective.

Although there are other *Phyllostachys* with similar colouring, I find this the most pleasing. It is tough, hardy and never shows stress, even when planted in dry woodland areas or on open boundaries. This cultivar and the species are widespread throughout

China where it inhabits the northern and central provinces that have the extremes of a continental climate, with the harshest winters and summers interspersed with intermittent monsoons. The culms are strong when dried and have many uses in the farming community – they are used to make tool handles, to weave and also for food, the early shoots being very sweet and tender.

In my garden, it stayed tight and tidy for ten or so years, after finding its feet near the base of the large overhanging pine. It then started to produce thicker and taller culms slightly away from the mother clump. It has never exceeded 3.5 m (11.5 ft.) and the culms are stout and relatively thick for their height. New culms are bloomy and a persistent felted white ring is present below the culm nodes, at least for the first growing season. Some of the culms also geniculate (zigzag) impressively at the base. The contrast between the gold of the grooves on the glossy green culms is more pronounced on younger, thicker culms. Older culms that have paled with age

can be used to contrast with the new culms or can also be removed.

Perhaps not as widely available as many of the other more robust *Phyllostachys* with similar culm colourings, I have listed this specimen here because of its reliability, quick growth and usefulness in smaller gardens. Its underground rhizomes are shallow and easier to remove than on some of the larger species, so it can easily be kept in place.

← The strong nodes on *Phyllostachys arcana* provide strength and make this species suitable for garden canes

Look out for

The true species *arcana* is generally taller and more vigorous, but is also even more lush and tolerant of the elements. It speedily forms screens, windbreaks or large meandering groves.

Phyllostachys aurea
Fishpole Bamboo or Golden Bamboo

This plant has stiff, upright culms with branching that is often lower at the base when compared to others within the genus. Culms on mature plants have compressed internodes that are quite low on the culm. New culms turn rich green from a blue-green colour and then age to a pale yellow-green. Usually tall, often clumping at first but likely to wander in time.

Culms: Maximum diameter 4.5 cm (1.75 in.)
Leaves: 13 × 2 cm (5 × 0.75 in.)

Hardiness and aspect
Min. −20°C (−4°F), zone 6
Full sun

Dimensions
Height: 4–8 m (13–26 ft.), average 6 m (20 ft.)
Spread: 1–3 m (3.3–10 ft.) in 10 years

Uses and combinations
Already widely used in gardens and landscapes in the West due to its ready availability, it is often used for

Checklist

✓ **Non-invasive**

✗ Short (0.3–1.5 m)

✗ Medium (1.5–3.5 m)

✓ **Tall (3.5 m +)**

✓ **Cold hardy**

✓ **Heat tolerant**

✓ **Drought tolerant**

✓ **Moisture tolerant**

✓ **Pots and containers**

✓ **Good for plant association**

✓ **Waterside planting**

✓ **Hedging, screening and windbreaks**

← Congested internodes on a strong culm of *Phyllostachys aurea*

hedging and planting by paths and driveways because of its reliable vertical habit. Nearby plantings of other structural plants with bold, darker leaves such as *Viburnum rhytidophyllum* or layered woody plants such as the many forms of *Viburnum plicatum* or *Cornus alternifolia* 'Argentea' are also well suited, but do not plant them so close together or you will lose their individuality.

In addition to its beauty, the popularity of this bamboo is reinforced by the fact that out of all the *Phyllostachys*, this species also performs admirably in subtropical and tropical environments.

Known as the 'Golden Bamboo', this name is highly misleading as the bamboo is actually green in all its parts. Older culms do turn yellow-green but not with the vitality of many of the other richly coloured *Phyllostachys* with true golden culms. Fishpole Bamboo is a better descriptive name, as the compressed lower culm internodes do provide a fine grip for such a tool. For this reason, this plant's culms have also been used for walking sticks and umbrella handles in China and

Japan. Other features of this bamboo are the very pronounced grooves known as sulci on alternate sides of each internode (identifiable on all *Phyllostachys*), as well as slight swellings below the nodes. The basal culm sheaths often persist and are best removed, particularly if they cover the congested beauty on the culms. This also applies to any low branching (more common on younger plants) and should always be done in the dormant season when there is no chance of damaging new culms. The foliage starts light and airy, becoming more plentiful with age and eventually producing an elegant but sturdy crown. In parts of the East it is known as *Taibo-chiku*, Phoenix Bamboo, as it rises from the ground and holds itself high with great dignity.

For all its beauty, as a simple green timber bamboo it does prefer an open aspect, preferably one with a rich, moisture-retentive soil, as it is not tolerant of deep shade or dry soil, where it will appear lacklustre and stunted. In warmer climates with good rainfall, *aurea* can form an aggressive colony, whereas in cooler locations it will remain tight at the base for many years and be shorter in structure.

I have two plants of this species in my garden. One is very grand at 8 m (26 ft.) tall, yet it is still refined at the base. It defies the adversity of its placement and holds itself up with some arrogance. It is situated in the lowest part of the garden where moisture is abundant, but nevertheless, its ability to withstand the frequent scathing winds has to be admired. The other specimen I have is planted close to a more vigorous *Phyllostachys bissetii* on a dry, unforgiving bank of poor soil and has been outperformed by its neighbour. It is ready for removal, looking sadder by the year with pale foliage and gaunt branching. This was all my mistake and not the fault of the plant.

Look out for

Phyllostachys aurea 'Flavescens Inversa' has rich green culms with yellow striping and is more suitable for smaller gardens, being slower to establish but requiring an open aspect.

Phyllostachys aurea 'Holochrysa'
Golden, Golden Bamboo

Generally forms a tight V-shape for many years in cool gardens. In warmer parts, it is more vertical and taller with well spaced culms. Known irritatingly as the 'Golden, Golden Bamboo', it is actually a golden form of the 'Golden Bamboo'! New blue-green culms ripen to butter-yellow, with the very old turning a rich, rust-stained gold. It has low branches that grow almost to the ground on compact plants.
Culms: Maximum diameter 4 cm (1.5 in.)
Leaves: 13 × 2 cm (5 × 0.75 in.)

Hardiness and aspect
Min. −20°C (−4°F), zone 6
Sun or very light shade

Dimensions
Height: 3.5–6 m (11.5–20 ft.), average 4 m (13 ft.)
Spread: 1–1.5 m (3.3–5 ft.) in 10 years

Uses and combinations
Similar to the previous *Phyllostachys aurea*, but if you are fortunate enough for it to stay compact,

Checklist

✓ **Non-invasive**

✗ Short (0.3–1.5 m)

✗ Medium (1.5–3.5 m)

✓ **Tall (3.5 m +)**

✓ **Cold hardy**

✓ **Heat tolerant**

✓ **Drought tolerant**

✗ Moisture tolerant

✓ **Pots and containers**

✓ **Good for plant association**

✓ **Waterside planting**

✓ **Hedging, screening and windbreaks**

← A young *Phyllostachys aurea* 'Holochrysa' acts as a useful evergreen background

associate planting is possible. Don't block the view of the culms, but plant combinations at the sides, for example arching *Phormium* and the shorter *Miscanthus* such as 'Kleine Silberspinne' or 'Little Kitten'. This bamboo colours well in pots and for its height is reasonably manageable. Thinning old culms and removing branches will help keep it in shape.

With a colour and habit that is distinct from all other bamboos, this bamboo has a subtle butter-yellow tone on the culms and paler leaves. The branches are short and rigid, holding the leaves stiffly, but lower branches need to be removed in the winter months so the beautiful colouring is visible. Culms can have heavily congested internodes at their base.

My garden specimen is still juvenile after fifteen years and it is the tightest *Phyllostachys* I have – it is perfectly healthy, but seemingly happy to remain in its youth. However, I am sure it will surprise me one day and display a few culms that are double the height and thickness of anything existing. In fact, I

← The beautiful colouring and congested internodes on a mature culm of *Phyllostachys aurea* 'Holochrysa'

have seen another plant half the age of mine that is already much taller with well spaced culms, growing in similar conditions. 'Holochrysa' is also noted by many to be more drought tolerant than the rest in this species, as a harsh environment actually improves the plant's colour. It always prefers an open aspect away from the shade.

← A butter-yellow three-year-old culm of *Phyllostachys aurea* 'Koi' with its deep green sulci

Look out for

Phyllostachys aurea 'Koi' is one of the most refined in this genus. New bloomy green culms develop a similar buttery colouring to 'Holochrysa', but with the addition of green grooves along the internodes. This plant usually has congested culms at the base and a low branching habit, so in an open aspect it will be shorter and more compact than others in this species.

Phyllostachys aurea 'Albovariegata' (syn. 'Variegata') is now thankfully returned from the dead. After flowering in the early 1990s it was deemed to be extinct, as all resulting seedlings and weak regenerated plants were green. However, seedlings were tracked down with variegated characteristics and this bamboo is now back in cultivation. It is hoped that the tight, short habit and the all over silvery, distant appearance will prove to be just as good as the original. It also used to be the most reliable *Phyllostachys*, showing true and obvious variegation of the leaves. However, my memories of the beauty of this bamboo two decades ago make the wait for new, mature plants all the more worthwhile.

Phyllostachys aureosulcata f. *aureocaulis*
Golden-Culmed Peking Bamboo, Golden Crook-Stem Bamboo

Elegant in habit, with rich golden culms that often tint a deep crimson-red, especially on new growth. Culms can geniculate (zigzag) and emerge a ghostly creamy-yellow, which will rapidly deepen to their true colouring. This plant is tidy and generally compact when compared to the true species. It has dark leaves with random thin yellow striping.

Culms: Maximum diameter 4 cm (1.6 in.)
Leaves: 17 × 1.5 cm (6.5 × 0.6 in.)

Hardiness and aspect
Min. −26°c (−15°F), zone 5
Sun or light shade

Checklist

✗ Non-invasive
✗ Short (0.3–1.5 m)
✗ Medium (1.5–3.5 m)
✓ **Tall (3.5 m +)**
✓ **Cold hardy**
✓ **Heat tolerant**
✓ **Drought tolerant**
✗ Moisture tolerant
✓ **Pots and containers**
✓ **Good for plant association**
✓ **Waterside planting**
✓ **Hedging, screening and windbreaks**

← The rich yellow culm colouring of *Phyllostachys aureosulcata* f. *aureocaulis*

Dimensions

Height: 4–7.5 m (13–24.6 ft.), average 5 m (16.5 ft.)
Spread: 1–2 m (4–10 ft.) in 10 years

Uses and combinations

A resilient plant that is useful almost anywhere, including as a windbreak or shelterbelt. However, its beauty means that it should have a prominent position, one that is never crowded and in full view. Perfect against a wall or dark fence when the colour and structure is framed from behind. Create a stepped layer of colour using the short waves of a generous planting of *Pleioblastus fortunei* and a deep purple leaved *Heuchera* in the foreground.

Phyllostachys aureosulcata and its naturally occurring forms are native to the eastern and northeastern provinces of China, a variable climate with harsh and prolonged winters. As a result, these bamboos have developed great strength and resilience through their development.

Highly recommended for cooler gardens, where its habit becomes refined and the colouring defines. This plant is one of the earliest in this genus to shoot in spring. Once established, it produces a good quantity of culms. The new, pale lemon-yellow culms push through the early colourful sheathing (a feature on its own), which has a soft olive-green colouring, streaked with pink and creamy-white. As the culms emerge into full light, they quickly develop their rich yellow pigment and reach their full height in only a few weeks. The long branches push outwards and are fully developed with unfolding leaves by mid-summer, giving an impressive layered effect to the upper culms. In bright sunlight, the new culms and branches turn orange with deep red tints. Very old culms mature to a rich tarnished gold and may also form very thin green stripes on the lower internodes.

The contrast between the dark green foliage and bright golden culms is, in my opinion, the most impressive quality overall. I have also seen this successfully used in large, broad containers. In this situation, the plant can almost be miniaturized, as the culms will be thinner and shorter but still stout, while the branches can be lightly trimmed and removed when necessary. Confinement also seems to enhance the delicious reddening of the culms and branches in strong sunlight.

← The red tints on these young culms and branches of *Phyllostachys aureosulcata* f. *aureocaulis* are enhanced by full sun

Look out for

Phyllostachys aureosulcata 'Lama Tempel' is said to randomly produce the culms of any of the other *aureosulcata* forms and cultivars, but I have yet to witness this. My plant has all golden culms and is not dissimilar to f. *aureocaulis* when young. On reaching maturity, the culms are a richer, burnished gold and new shoots have a deeper pink sheathing. Green striae are more prevalent on the lower parts of the culms and the whole plant is also stocky and shorter in height. Branches are more congested at the top, as the culms taper quickly, making the internodes shorter. Very rare, but worth hunting down.

Phyllostachys aureosulcata f. *spectabilis*
Green Grooved Bamboo

This plant has intense, custard yellow culms with dark green sulci, while young culms can be red tinted from the sun. New (pale lemon-yellow) culms have a white bloom below each node and emerge from pink and green striped sheathing, while zigzag shapes appear on some. Dark, glossy foliage is supported by strong vertical culms. It is more compact in cool areas, taking longer to mature but is always visually fresh.

Culms: Maximum diameter 4.5 cm (1.75 in.)
Leaves: 17 × 1.5 cm (6.5 × 0.6 in.)

Hardiness and aspect

Min. −26°C (−15°F), zone 5
Sun or light shade

Checklist

✗ Non-invasive

✗ Short (0.3–1.5 m)

✗ Medium (1.5–3.5 m)

✓ **Tall (3.5 m +)**

✓ **Cold hardy**

✓ **Heat tolerant**

✓ **Drought tolerant**

✗ Moisture tolerant

✓ **Pots and containers**

✓ **Good for plant association**

✓ **Waterside planting**

✓ **Hedging, screening and windbreaks**

← A deep red young culm in midsummer

Dimensions

Height: 4–9 m (13–30 ft.), average 6 m (20 ft.)

Spread: 1–3 m (3.3–10 ft.) in 10 years

Uses and combinations

This plant is as versatile as it gets – it can be used for screens, windbreaks, specimen planting, woodland areas and large mixed borders. Very effective in winter gardens with white stemmed birch or *Rubus* or yellow flowered *Mahonia*, with its spiky horizontal greenery and dark evergreen ground cover of the glossy *Rubus tricolor*.

Undoubtedly one of the most superior of ornamental garden plants, this never fails to impress. This bamboo is number one on my list of best bamboos, simply because if I was ever limited to just one bamboo, this would be it. The contrast between the gold and green colouring on the culms is very pronounced, as is the orange-red tinting on new culms. Culms emerge as a pale yellow colour, quickly turning to custard or mustard yellow and have a rough, almost pig-skin tactile quality. This trait makes them (as well as the rest of the species) easy to identify. The dark, shiny leaves have random streaks of creamy-white on their uppersides and are matte blue-green on their undersides, which provides a two-tone effect when they are fluttering in the breeze.

A glut of tight and tidy medium height culms will be produced quickly. Depending on location, at maturity this plant is capable of producing culms that are twice as tall and thick. This bamboo could be a nuisance in dry gardens, as the dense overhead canopy of branches and leaves cast the rainfall outwards beyond the clump below, forcing the rhizome and roots to reach out for refreshment. Having said that, I have never seen a specimen out of control – even my twenty years old specimen, which is planted in a somewhat dry and unforgiving place, is only 2 m (6.5 ft.) across at the base. In my opinion, its colouring is better in cool climates, where the density of the culms can shine brightly as a whole. This plant is never phased by cold winds, hot summers, drought or impoverished soils.

This plant is also at the top of the list due to its proven cold hardiness. It grows admirably in zone 5 as a refined and tight clump, shooting early and forming good structure quickly. It is more aggressive in zones 7 – 10, with wider spaced culms that are also much taller and thicker. This species is already widely planted worldwide as it responds well to all sorts of conditions, a good reason for it to be a popular choice.

← The natural zigzag shaping on some of the culms of *Phyllostachys aureosulcata*

Look out for

The species *aureosulcata* has inverse culm colouring of dusky green with gold sulci. Nearly always more vigorous than f. *spectabilis*, it forms a quick windbreak or screen. *Phyllostachys aureosulcata* 'Argus' has spectacular golden culms and longitudinal green striae that is not just restricted to the grooves of the culm. Similarly, orange-red tints show an equal vigour and hardiness to f. *spectabilis*. 'Argus' is the most hardy and reliable bamboo with this colouring, being a good substitute for the often requested *Bambusa multiplex* 'Alphonse Karr' or *Bambusa vulgaris* 'Vittata', neither of which are cold hardy.

Phyllostachys bambusoides 'Allgold' (syn. *'Holochrysa'*)
All Gold Bamboo

This plant's deep, orange-yellow culms have the richest and darkest tone amongst the yellow culm bamboos. Often forming a grove wider than it is high, this plant has quite a stocky habit, but is generally slow and compact in cool gardens. The dark greenery on the long and loose branches form individual layers, but their weight may cause older culms to slightly arch outwards eventually.

"With sunlight behind, the culms appear almost translucent."

Checklist

- ✗ Non-invasive
- ✗ Short (0.3–1.5 m)
- ✗ Medium (1.5–3.5 m)
- ✓ **Tall (3.5 m +)**
- ✓ **Cold hardy**
- ✓ **Heat tolerant**
- ✓ **Drought tolerant**
- ✗ Moisture tolerant
- ✓ **Pots and containers**
- ✓ **Good for plant association**
- ✓ **Waterside planting**
- ✓ **Hedging, screening and windbreaks**

← A well thinned stand of *Phyllostachys bambusoides* 'Allgold' with a simple log seat

← New culms of *Phyllostachys bambusoides* 'Allgold' can turn burnished orange in sunlight

Culms: Maximum diameter 6 cm (2.4 in.)
Leaves: 15 × 3.5 cm (6 × 1.4 in.)

Hardiness and aspect
Min. −15°C (5°F), zone 7
Sun or light shade

Dimensions
Height: 4–9 m (13–39 ft.), average 6 m (20 ft.)
Spread: 1–3 m (3.3–10 ft.) in 10 years

Uses and combinations
This plant requires no additional clutter, as its individual beauty is more than a feast for the eyes. However, if you must, an open and thinned grove can be underplanted with a wide variety of other plants, as the well-spaced overhead branch system does allow good light and moisture through. Try *Uncinia rubra* (red hook sedge) from New Zealand and the odd *Hosta*, which when established will be more drought tolerant than you think. If the bamboo stays in a tight clump, surround it with a broad circle of the green *Hakonechloa macra* (Hakone grass).

In one of my previous nursery catalogues, I offered the following description for this bamboo: "Another deep golden, almost orange culmed bamboo. Well spaced, eventually tall with thick culms and a sparse branch and leaf arrangement, allowing the colour to be seen from distant galaxies." You may think this is a slight exaggeration, but it certainly highlights the point about the vivid culm colouring. With sunlight behind, the culms appear almost translucent. With sunlight in front, they seem to absorb all light and glow with a phosphorescent quality.

Known as 'Allgold' in the United States, I have to admit I prefer this name to its supposedly correct cultivar name of 'Holochrysa'. It saves confusion with *Phyllostachys aurea* 'Holochrysa', which is altogether different in appearance. The true species *bambusoides*

is native to many provinces in China and all the forms and cultivars of *bambusoides* also shoot later in the year than most bamboos. This late shooting has the effect of making them slower to mature, mainly due to the fact that late shooting means fewer shoots annually.

To our advantage, 'Allgold' is the first of the species to shoot, giving it the edge in terms of speed of maturity. New shoots appear and are protected by brazenly spotted and blotched sheathing, while new, smooth culms emerge quickly as the sheaths are discarded. As with many golden culmed bamboos, there is often sunburn-like reddening on early new growth, which has been noted particularly around the nodes and lower branches on 'Allgold'. Long horizontal branches develop quite large leaves when compared to those of the species, some blessed with creamy-white stripes.

In terms of habit, 'Allgold' can be very variable as it can be highly affected by altitude, latitude and the resultant cooler or warmer climate. It is frustratingly slow and compact in the coolest of gardens, but it can reach very open and large proportions in warm or sheltered spots. It does, however, relish an open position and hates being crowded.

← Stout green culms of *Phyllostachys bambusoides*

Look out for
Phyllostachys bambusoides, the all green species. It is larger in habit, bold in appearance and is the archetypal timber bamboo of China. It needs plenty of room to perform properly.

"Always admired, irrespective of size. The colouring never fails to impress."

Checklist

- ✗ Non-invasive
- ✗ Short (0.3–1.5 m)
- ✗ Medium (1.5–3.5 m)
- ✓ **Tall (3.5 m +)**
- ✓ **Cold hardy**
- ✓ **Heat tolerant**
- ✓ **Drought tolerant**
- ✗ Moisture tolerant
- ✓ **Pots and containers**
- ✓ **Good for plant association**
- ✓ **Waterside planting**
- ✓ **Hedging, screening and windbreaks**

← The sun-kissed, bright golden culms of *Phyllostachys bambusoides* 'Castillonis'

← The inverse culm colouring of *Phyllostachys bambusoides* 'Castillonis Inversa'

Phyllostachys bambusoides 'Castillonis'
Castillon Bamboo

Eventually grows into thick and tall golden culms with deep green alternate grooves (sulci), although the contrast between these two colours is more pronounced on the smooth young culms. Stately and vertical with high branches holding creamy, pinstriped green leaves.

Culms: Maximum diameter 6.5 cm (2.5 in.)
Leaves: 15 × 3.5 cm (6 × 1.4 in.)

Hardiness and aspect

Min. −18°C (0°F), zone 6
Sun or light shade.

Dimensions

Height: 4–10 m (13–22 ft.), average 6 m (20 ft.)
Spread: 75 cm–2 m (2.5–6.5 ft.) in 10 years

Uses and combinations

Too robust for a pot, this needs a place in the ground. My plant is complemented at its base by a *Hedera helix* 'Ivalace' – the combination of the majestic culms rising through the tumble of dark greenery is simple but effective. This is a fine individual, so don't lose it within a crowd of other plants.

This cultivar is by far the most popular within the species, as it is much in demand. It will start life slowly – with my plant, only one or two shoots were produced annually, but over ten years the clump developed. My specimen formed a clump of well–spaced, sturdy culms for eighteen years, but in its nineteenth year, it started to run and produced a new culm some 2 m (6.5 ft.) away from the parent. This is the natural propagation method of any *Phyllostachys*. Since that first wayward culm, two or three other offspring colonies have been produced at a distance

and the whole diameter of the base is now 3 m (10 ft.). It is worth noting that it took over two decades for this growth to happen. My *Phyllostachys vivax* f. *aureocaulis* covered the same amount of ground in half that time, as its earlier shooting time and more plentiful production allowed for it to mature more quickly.

The new, buttery yellow culms of 'Castillonis' rise from dark sheathing in midsummer, forming branches when the culms reach their final height. It is always a worry as to whether the leaves will be produced in time for winter, though they nearly always are. Leaf production is an affirmation that the branches and the tops of the culms have ripened sufficiently to withstand the elements without die-back.

Look out for

Phyllostachys bambusoides 'Castillonis Inversa' is exactly as the name suggests, having inverse culm colouring to 'Castillonis' – dark green culms with mustard yellow grooves. Usually smaller in stature but my plant proved otherwise, reaching the proportions of my 'Castillonis' in less than half the time. You have probably learned by now that bamboos have minds of their own.

Phyllostachys bambusoides 'Kawadana' is a rare offering and should you wish to acquire it, you will have to start at the bottom of the waiting list. It has subtle creamy-yellow striped leaves, pale green culms and pale yellow striping at head height. Nearly always tidy and tight, thus making propagation almost impossible.

Checklist

✗ Non-invasive

✗ Short (0.3–1.5 m)

✗ Medium (1.5–3.5 m)

✓ Tall (3.5 m +)

✓ Cold hardy

✓ Heat tolerant

✓ Drought tolerant

✗ Moisture tolerant

✓ Pots and containers

✓ Good for plant association

✓ Waterside planting

✓ Hedging, screening and windbreaks

← A strong green culm of *Phyllostachys bissetii*

Phyllostachys bissetii
Bisset's Bamboo or David Bisset's Bamboo

Tall, thick and upright culms change from dark green to pale olive, forming a large, dense grove. A dark mass of fresh, shiny leaves will emerge unscathed from the harshest of winters.
Culms: Maximum diameter 5 cm (2 in.)
Leaves: 9 × 1.5 cm (3.5 × 0.6 in.)

Hardiness and aspect
Min. −22°c (−8°f), zone 6
Sun or light shade

Dimensions
Height: 5–12 m (16.5–30 ft.), average 7 m (23 ft.)

Spread: 1.5–4 m (5–13 ft.) in 10 years

Uses and combinations

Forms an indomitable hedge or large screen that will act as a dark background for any other planting scheme. For those of you with wide, open spaces, I would suggest this as one of the fastest to provide shelter.

This rewarding bamboo has been known throughout the United States since the middle of the twentieth century, but it is only a recent introduction into Europe. It has already been used widely, as word has spread about its tolerance regarding the adversities of a cold climate.

One of many green culmed *Phyllostachys*, it can prove difficult to identify as a youngster, however the pale yellow-green culm sheaths protecting the new growth are usually stained a pale wine-red. The darkest culms emerge quickly and are also great in number, making maturity speedy and impressive, with dense layers of deep green glossy leaves that billow and sway in the wind. In my garden, I have a dense screen covering some 12 m (40 ft.) at the base. This started as three young nursery plants some twenty or so years ago, planted to divide the nursery from the garden. The grove is now well over twice the height of a 4 m (13 ft.) polythene tunnel and the tops of the bamboo are visible from the distant fields. It catches the full blow of the prevailing southwesterly wind and never looks beaten or scarred by the exposure. At the end of one of the large fields, there is a small spinney used for rearing pheasants in readiness for the winter shooting season. I have known the birds to flock to my huge stand of *bissetii* for sanctuary as soon as they hear shots in the distance.

I also have another plant on less friable and poorer soil. Although the plant has a much shorter and tighter clump, it still creates an effective 5 m (16.5 ft.) screen from the neighbouring garden.

Together, these plants prove the point that appearance and habit can be governed by the difference in soil quality, as these plants are very close in age and location.

Look out for

There are far too many green culmed *Phyllostachys* to mention, but *Phyllostachys viridiglaucescens* is well tried and tested, being one of the earliest introductions to the West. Equal in vigour to *bissetii*, with masses of new culm growth annually, but it is generally a paler green in all its parts. When planted as part of a screen with *bissetii*, you will realize just how much the colour green can vary!

Phyllostachys iridescens
Red Sheath Bamboo

One of the easiest *Phyllostachys* to identify. Its bloomy blue-green new culms are protected by vivid red-brown mottled sheathing and topped with large, pendulous, rainbow coloured blades. Old culms come to have a beautiful vertical striping when mature, ranging from yellow to dark green and faint purple-brown. Eventually forms a tall grove of well spaced culms.

Culms: Maximum diameter 8 cm (3 in.)
Leaves: 10 × 1.5 cm (4 × 0.6 in.)

"New culms grew to their full height in just six short weeks."

Checklist

- ✗ Non-invasive
- ✗ Short (0.3–1.5 m)
- ✗ Medium (1.5–3.5 m)
- ✓ **Tall (3.5 m +)**
- ✓ **Cold hardy**
- ✓ **Heat tolerant**
- ✓ **Drought tolerant**
- ✗ Moisture tolerant
- ✗ Pots and containers
- ✓ **Good for plant association**
- ✓ **Waterside planting**
- ✓ **Hedging, screening and windbreaks**

← New culms of *Phyllostachys iridescens*

← Inside a grove of *Phyllostachys iridescens*

Hardiness and aspect

Min. −18°C (0°F), zone 6
Sun or light shade

Dimensions

Height: 6–12 m (20–40 ft.), average 8 m (26 ft.)
Spread: 1–2.5 m (3.3–10 ft.) in 10 years

Uses and combinations

Needs to be appreciated, as it is outstandingly beautiful and requires no companionship. Plant it as a focal point in the centre of a large island bed, leaving the occasional vista clear to allow viewing of the new shoots, or use it as a centrepiece in an open glade within light woodland.

This bamboo is limited to the eastern coastal provinces of China and north and south of Shanghai in the wild, although it has been planted widely throughout the rest of the country for construction purposes and also its prized sweet shoots. In contrast, it is infuriatingly rare in the West and is often incorrectly named or displayed when offered for sale. Its ability to mature rapidly from wispy juvenile plants means it is difficult to propagate, with older plants resenting the disturbance. The dark red-brown new shoots with their colourful wispy blades very quickly develop into bloomy blue-green culms with high branching. Culms eventually pale and in subsequent years develop yellow, green and purple-brown striping along the length of the internodes, while some culms can also slightly zigzag at the base. It is the the stocky, timber-like structure that makes this bamboo so appealing.

New culms will stay together for a few years after planting, but as thicker rhizomes are produced, thicker culms will appear with more spacing, usually tapering quickly at the top. After many years, the clump will enlarge to the point where it is able to support new culms maturing to 3–4 m (10–13 ft.) and rising above all the existing growth. After eighteen years here in my garden, my *iridescens* did just that, when the new 12 m (40 ft.) culms grew to their full height in just six short weeks.

Look out for

Phyllostachys violascens is more widely planted but not as refined as *iridescens*. It is fast to mature and will romp through and around anything in its path. It also has even, bold yellow and purple striping on old culms.

Phyllostachys dulcis is known as the sweet shoot bamboo. It is comparable in habit and strength to *iridescens* in warmer locations, but in cool gardens it will struggle to mature. Culms are a deep shining green, well spaced and very tall, while new shoots are an unmistakable very pale, creamy green.

Phyllostachys nigra
Black Bamboo

With unique, jet-black culms when mature, these emerge green and tone to their lustrous ebony colouring during a one to three year period. The colouring will be quicker to ripen in sunlight, but beware as there is also some clonal variation and some forms are better than others. In cool gardens it is stout, usually clumping and compact, but in warmer locations it will be taller and more open in habit, with colouring sometimes not showing as vividly. It has small leaves for the genus that are

Checklist

✗ Non-invasive
✗ Short (0.3–1.5 m)
✗ Medium (1.5–3.5 m)
✓ **Tall (3.5 m +)**
✓ **Cold hardy**
✓ **Heat tolerant**
✓ **Drought tolerant**
✗ Moisture tolerant
✓ **Pots and containers**
✓ **Good for plant association**
✓ **Waterside planting**
✓ **Hedging, screening and windbreaks**

← A jet-black three year old culm with a pale circular sheath scar just below the node

sometimes bleached at the tips during winter and early spring.

Culms: Maximum diameter 5 cm (2 in.)
Leaves: 8 × 1.3 cm (3 × 0.5 in.)

Hardiness and aspect

Min. −18°c (0°f), zone 6
Full sun

Dimensions

Height: 4–12 m (13–40 ft.), average 6 m (20 ft.)
Spread: 75 cm–1.5 m (2.5–5 ft.) in 10 years

Uses and combinations

The black culm colouring is very versatile and can be combined with almost anything. I prefer the rich purple tones of a spiky *Cordyline* and the large fresh greenery of a *Fatsia* with a splash of gold or variegation from some low bamboos such as

Pleioblastus viridistriatus or *Pleioblastus fortunei*. I have also seen it used successfully in pots but only with hard work, as it requires much devotion to maintain the correct balance of moisture, feeding and pruning to keep it in shape.

This ubiquitous plant is still as fashionable now as it ever has been, not just in the West but also in China and Japan, where it is also widely planted as an ornamental. However, enquiries still abound for a short black bamboo, or one with larger leaves, so I have to say at this point that there is only one black bamboo, and it has no variety. There are one or two selected clones, but they still have the same structure and general appearance.

Green culms erupt initially from the pale pink and cinnamon coloured shoots, while the black culm colouring or pigment develops with age due to its exposure to light.

This species flowered in the early 1900s and today there is some variability in colouring depending on your stock source. When purchasing, assess or ask about the plant's one year old culms. If they show good blackening, particularly towards the end of the summer, then the clone is a good one – otherwise avoid. It is almost always very compact and slow in cool gardens, but can be aggressive when warmer.

Compact plants tend to have a slightly arching V-shaped habit, while plants with thicker and taller culms will be much more vertical, arching only slightly at the top. Good clones will produce glossy boot-polish black culms. As they age, the culm sheath scars below each node will also whiten for a very striking effect.

For all its beauty and individuality, *nigra* does have two less than favourable qualities. One is that on compact plants, the culms branch almost to the base so removal is necessary to appreciate the colouring. This also exposes more of the culms to the sunlight, speeding up the transition from green to black. Secondly, the small, delicate looking leaves can scorch in extreme weather. This is a normal characteristic and admittedly not unattractive (except when kept in containers – you will be glad to see the new growth appear in summer), but you must know what to expect.

Look out for

Phyllostachys nigra 'Fulva' (syn *P. fulva*) is rarely available. The culms vary from a rich dark brown on the newer culms to a glossy tawny colour on the older ones. Short, compact and paler in leaf, it relishes an open aspect.

Phyllostachys nigra 'Boryana'
Snakeskin Bamboo or Leopard Bamboo

Very variable according to location, as with *P. nigra*, but generally more vigorous. One year old green culms gradually become blotched and stained, taking on a dark shiny brown colour over a two to three year period. Compared to its stature the leaves are quite small, creating a more vertical habit.

Culms: Maximum diameter 10 cm (4 in.)
Leaves: 9 × 1.5 cm (3.5 × 0.6 in.)

Hardiness and aspect
Min. −18°C (0°F), zone 6
Sun or light shade

"During the second and third years leopard-skin patterns emerge."

Checklist

✗ Non-invasive

✗ Short (0.3–1.5 m)

✗ Medium (1.5–3.5 m)

✓ Tall (3.5 m +)

✓ Cold hardy

✓ Heat tolerant

✓ Drought tolerant

✓ Moisture tolerant

✓ Pots and containers

✓ Good for plant association

✓ Waterside planting

✓ Hedging, screening and windbreaks

← The spotted and blotched culm from *Phyllostachys nigra* 'Boryana'

Dimensions

Height: 5–15 m (16.5–50 ft.), average 7 m (23 ft.)
Spread: 1–4 m (3.3–13 ft.) in 10 years

Uses and combinations

This and *Phyllostachys nigra* are two bamboos that retain their dark culm colouring when dried, proving themselves useful for floral decorations. As a garden plant, like many in the *Phyllostachys* group, it deserves its own prominent setting. The dark culms lend themselves to pale companion plantings of low ground cover, such as *Hedera helix* 'Buttercup', a bright golden leaved ivy, or hummocks of the fine silvery Japanese sedge, *Carex morrowii* 'Variegata', which performs well in shade.

Not known in the wild, this brassy cultivar is said to originate in Japan where it is used widely for its reliable architectural qualities. It can be frustratingly slow in cool gardens, forming a tight V-shaped bush that needs careful thinning to prevent crowding of the culms.

Give it a little warmth, keep it away from exposure and it will respond quickly, replacing the congested starter plant with tall, thick vertical culms. I have never seen it behave rampantly, but it does need room eventually.

'Boryana' prefers an open aspect where the culm colouring will show quickly. New olive-green culms show only slight blotching by the end of the first year, but during the second and third seasons distinct leopard-skin patterns emerge. Very old culms often have more dark brown colouring than green, and so the mixture of new, maturing and old colourings provides much interest.

Like *Phyllostachys nigra*, it has small leaves for the genus and also branches low down on immature plants. Branches should be removed during the dormant winter months so you can best appreciate the colouring. In my garden, this plant has never performed to its true ability because it has been crowded out by surrounding small trees and other bamboos, which has been a lesson learned.

Look out for

Phyllostachys nigra 'Megurochiku' has green culms that develop black colouring purely in the alternate grooves on the internodes. As the black colouring develops over two or three years, the green turns a paler bright yellow-ochre. Best in an open aspect for quick colouration.

Phyllostachys nigra f. *henonis*
Henon Bamboo

Erect and tall in habit with green culms, the foamy mass of delicate pale leaves in the high canopy makes this an impressive foliage bamboo. New culms have a temporarily pale colour, whereas the old turn yellow-green, offering contrast. Minor tip bleaching on the leaves is common but uniform, which adds to the appearance.

Culms: Maximum diameter 10 cm (4 in.)
Leaves: 9 × 1.5 cm (3.5 × 0.6 in.)

Hardiness and aspect

Min. −26°C (−15°F), zone 5
Sun or light shade

Dimensions

Height: 6–20 m (20–65.5 ft.), average 8 m (26 ft.)
Spread: 1.5–3.5 m (5–11.5 ft.) in 10 years

Uses and combinations

This plant's robustness lends it to individual specimen planting or mixing with bamboos of similar vigour, such as in hedging and screening. As with many of the green bamboos, it forms a pure and bold architectural feature, evoking visions of the Orient.

From an evolutionary perspective, this bamboo should really be the true *nigra* species, however the black *Phyllostachys nigra* was discovered first and so f. *henonis* was relegated to second place, which is quite uncommon for a green bamboo. Native to vast areas of China, the nature of the variable climate and conditions in these regions proves the versatility and adaptability of this fine bamboo.

Widely used in larger landscape settings, this bamboo is also much favoured in the cooler and more mountainous regions of Japan. Few bamboos can match the size and performance of f. *henonis* in cool locations.

> *"Very thick and tall culms can appear quite suddenly."*

Checklist

✗ Non-invasive
✗ Short (0.3–1.5 m)
✗ Medium (1.5–3.5 m)
✓ **Tall (3.5 m+)**
✓ **Cold hardy**
✓ **Heat tolerant**
✓ **Drought tolerant**
✗ Moisture tolerant
✓ **Pots and containers**
✓ **Good for plant association**
✓ **Waterside planting**
✓ **Hedging, screening and windbreaks**

← Detail on a new culm of *Phyllostachys nigra* f. *henonis*

New culms emerge with their dusty powdery coating, first turning rich green then paling with age. Very thick and tall culms can appear quite suddenly from developing plants, sometimes leaning or falling down because of the lack of supporting structures below. It does at least show, however, that this bamboo has a strong propensity and desire to grow.

As a general rule, this species will mostly keep in bounds as agressive behaviour is usually the exception. However, its potential height and foliage mass means it will inevitably cast shade, so think carefully where you place it.

Look out for

Phyllostachys nuda is highly ornamental, vigorous and ultra-hardy with edible shoots. It has very dark green emerging culms that often zigzag at the base. Silvery blooms persist below the nodes for a ringed effect. This plant needs space as it forms a large and dense grove, but is usually shorter than most other green species.

"Has a strong, upright and always well manicured structure."

Checklist

✗ Non-invasive

✗ Short (0.3–1.5 m)

✗ Medium (1.5–3.5 m)

✓ **Tall (3.5 m +)**

✓ **Cold hardy**

✓ **Heat tolerant**

✓ **Drought tolerant**

✗ Moisture tolerant

✓ **Pots and containers**

✓ **Good for plant association**

✓ **Waterside planting**

✓ **Hedging, screening and windbreaks**

→ With its tidy habit, *Phyllostachys propinqua* is well suited to a small garden

Phyllostachys propinqua
Withered Sheath Bamboo

Has a tendency to clump and remain vertical, eventually forming new colonies close by. The leaves appear narrow as they curl slightly inwards from edge to edge in a fluted manner. Fresh green culms pale to an ochre-yellow and are structurally robust, especially at the prominent nodes, enabling them to remain strong and unbending.

Culms: Maximum diameter 5 cm (2 in.)

Leaves: 12 × 1.3 cm (4.75 × 0.5 in.)

Hardiness and aspect

Min. −23°C (−10°F), zone 6

Sun or light shade

Dimensions
Height: 4–9 m (13–30 ft.), average 6 m (20 ft.)
Spread: 75 cm–1.5 m (2.5–5 ft.) in 10 years

Uses and combinations
Although beefy in habit, this rarely reaches huge proportions and is easily used in a smaller garden. The high branches allow for good viewing of the well structured basal clump and it make an impressive stand-alone feature. A few randomly sized beach pebbles strewn at the base will show the leaf shadow from above.

New culms appear during mid summer and are protected by olive-green, bronze tinted sheathing that is delicately flecked with dark spotting. Green culms with noticeable nodes expand quickly upwards and unleash their long branches outwards in an umbrella-like style. The leaves are shiny green on the top side and a paler blue-green matte on the reverse, tapering to fine points and glistening in the light with their slight twisting and curling.

I gave a young *propinqua* plant to a friend who required additional screening from the neighbouring garden. Being a conifer nurseryman, his garden is full of formality and riots of rich winter colour, but the bamboo unexpectedly slots into place amongst the surrounding plants with great ease. It does the job intended and as a bonus, also detracts from a nearby compost heap. Apart from last year when one easily removed rhizome pushed towards the lawn, this bamboo has stayed well within its bounds.

Look out for
Phyllostachys heteroclada 'Straight Stem' also has a tidy vertical habit. It will mature in a more open structure than *propinqua*, but is of similar height. New culms are entirely covered with a ghostly, waxy pale bloom, providing a silvery sheen. Also commonly known as the water bamboo, it is tolerant of boggy conditions due to air channels in the rhizomes.

Phyllostachys vivax f. *aureocaulis*
Golden Chinese Timber Bamboo and Golden Vivax Bamboo

Magnificent, tall golden culms with random, green longitudinal striae that often create a barcode effect and tend to appear low down on the culms. Eventually very vertical with long internodes resulting in evenly spaced branches and mid-green leaves, sometimes with the odd fine creamy-yellow stripe. The well-spaced culms usually need room to perform, but they have been known to break the rules and remain tight.

Culms: Maximum diameter 13 cm (5 in.)
Leaves: Average 13 x 2.5 cm (5 xi in.)

Hardiness and aspect
Min. −21°c (−5°F), zone 6
Sun

Dimensions
Height: 6–20 m (20–65.6 ft.), average 8 m (26 ft.)

"If you are looking to make a quick impression, choose this."

Checklist

✗ Non-invasive

✗ Short (0.3–1.5 m)

✗ Medium (1.5–3.5 m)

✓ **Tall (3.5 m +)**

✓ **Cold hardy**

✓ **Heat tolerant**

✓ **Drought tolerant**

✗ Moisture tolerant

✗ Pots and containers

✓ **Good for plant association**

✓ **Waterside planting**

✓ **Hedging, screening and windbreaks**

→ The green barcoding effect on *Phyllostachys vivax* f. *aureocaulis*

Spread: 1–3 m (3.3–10 ft.) in 10 years

Uses and combinations

This plant is very bold with strong architectural quality. It is superb for creating reflections on large ponds and/or lakes, but is useless in pots as it needs room to grow. However, it is fine in large raised beds if thinned regularly and given additional water and nutrients. My plant is backed by the leafy ×*Hibanobambusa tranquillans* 'Shiroshima', with its

branches of variegation poking through the golden culms of the *Phyllostachys*. At the base, I have the short nodding flowers of *Persicaria amplexicaulis* 'Inverleith' (syn. 'Pendula') and a gold leaved *Rubus cockburnianus* 'Goldenvale' randomly popping up amidst the culms with its pure, winter-white thorny stems.

Although all the *Phyllostachys* mentioned so far have their individual charms, features and habits, this plant is undoubtedly one of the best. I am frequently asked which bamboos provide tall and thick culms more quickly than others – although some can exceed this bamboo in height and culm girth, choose this if you are looking to make a quick impression.

This bamboo is surely one of the most rewarding and ornamental of all the hardy bamboos suited to cool gardens. Pale, buttery yellow culms emerge from dark, vividly spotted sheathing and the speed of upward development is always impressive, particularly at the height of summer when the cracking of sheaths can be heard as the culms expand. The green striping near the base of the culms is quite random. On some culms it may not be present apart from a few faint green lines here and there, while on others the striping is more pronounced, with broad, vertical green bars or a combination of thin and thick stripes in varying number. I have also seen culms that are completely green on one side and gold on the other. On this plant the well-spaced branching curves slightly downwards, with the leaves casting flickering shadows on the culms below.

My plant has provided me with a fine open grove, leaning slightly forward and away from a huge weeping willow behind it. It greets all with its showiness, making all who pass bow in respect as they try to avoid the overhanging culms and branches. It is separated from the shingle path by a thick, treated timber edge that is 25 cm (0.9 ft.) deep and protrudes 6 cm (0.15 ft.) above the surface. In a friend's garden, there is a plant the same age as mine that has remained in a tight clump, so much so that it is almost possible to encircle the base with my arms. My plant is 3 m (10 ft.) across at the base.

This fine, golden bamboo has one other unique quality, in that it can randomly produce a culm or two of the (supposed) form *Phyllostachys vivax* f. *huanvenzhu* with green culms and golden sulci. Not a reversion as you may think, as in fact both of these plants could be genetically the same, even though they are different in appearance.

Look out for

Phyllostachys vivax f. *huanvenzhu* is a real peculiarity. As stated previously, this can appear randomly as a part of *Phyllostachys vivax* f. *aureocaulis* – this process can also happen in reverse. With its strong shiny green culms and yellow sulci, this form is actually more likely to show culms of the golden form at any time. There is never any need to remove either of these, as the two colours will happily coexist without either dominating the other. You would be unlucky to purchase a plant that at some point didn't do this – the effect is quite striking and unusual.

← *Phyllostachys vivax* f. *huanvenzhu inversa*

Phyllostachys vivax is the true species that after many years can reach dizzying heights with its thick green culms. *Phyllostachys vivax* f. *huanvenzhu inversa* is the opposite of f. *huanvenzhu* with its golden culms and rich green sulci. It is a possible rival for the much sought after *Phyllostachys bambusoides* 'Castillonis', although the bonus is that *vivax* forms can mature in half the time of *bambusoides* forms. *Phyllostachys vivax* f. *huanvenzhu inversa* is a relative newcomer to the bamboo scene and is said to be more stable than its opposite. All these forms perform brilliantly in cool gardens.

> *"A rounded, tidy habit will be formed."*

Checklist

✗ Non-invasive

✗ Short (0.3–1.5 m)

✓ **Medium (1.5–3.5 m)**

✗ Tall (3.5 m +)

✓ **Cold hardy**

✓ **Heat tolerant**

✓ **Drought tolerant**

✗ Moisture tolerant

✓ **Pots and containers**

✓ **Good for plant association**

✓ **Waterside planting**

✓ **Hedging, screening and windbreaks**

→ The finely variegated leaves of *Pleioblastus chino* f. *elegantissimus*

Pleioblastus chino f. *elegantissimus*
Variegated Bitter Bamboo

Short and elegant in habit, with a silvery glow when viewed from a distance. It also boasts masses of long, thin finely variegated leaves, which are artistically striped with varying widths and lengths of silver-white and pale lime-green.

Culms: Maximum diameter 1.25 cm (0.5 in.)

Leaves: 9 × 0.5 cm (3.5 × 0.2 in.)

Hardiness and aspect

Min. −18°c (0°F), zone 6
Sun or part shade

Dimensions

Height: 1–2 m (3.3–6.5 ft.), average 1.5 m (5 ft.)
Spread: 75 cm–1.5 m (2.5–5 ft.) in 10 years

Uses and combinations

Its short stature lends itself to mixed borders and it also performs well in pots, being tolerant of medium to long-term confinement. The best specimen I have seen was isolated in light shade, but was also backed by the darker, larger leaved *Pseudosasa japonica* 'Tsutsumiana'. For colour association in a small border, use blues and reds – the evergreen *Liriope muscari* with its small blue pokers and the early, deep orange-red flowers of *Geum* 'Mrs J. Bradshaw' are also bright and long-lived. For a lengthy display, try *Skimmia japonica* 'Rubella'.

With the exception of one or two of the taller species, all the *Pleioblastus* plants originate from Japan. All, in their own way, provide an oriental ambience. Many are simple foliage plants that lack the substantial culm structure of the Chinese timber bamboos and as a result are short and versatile, good for lower level planting.

This bamboo, although short in bamboo terms, grows to medium height amongst the *Pleioblastus* but it does take time to get there. Young nursery plants often look slim and gangling as it is not until the rhizome has recovered (a year or two after propagation) that anything remotely substantial is seen on top. Beyond this point, new slender culms will rise through the wispy juvenile growth, opening sparsely in leaf during the first season. In subsequent years, more leaves are produced, which lightly arches the culms. With this continual production of vertical and weeping culms, a rounded and tidy habit will naturally be formed.

As with nearly all *Pleioblastus*, this bamboo can be invasive when it reaches maturity, but fear not – the rhizomes are shallow, so a little bit of foraging will keep the bamboo firmly in check. This is a fine choice for containers if given a little shelter in winter either against a wall or in a cold glasshouse to stop excessive desiccation, should the pot be badly frosted. A friend kindly loaned me a large tub of this bamboo many moons ago, for use in an exhibition. A beautiful specimen with good shape and colour, it remained naughtily in my possession for almost a decade. During that time, the plant never received additional fertilizer (just water) and never flinched at the lack of attention.

Look out for

Pleioblastus chino 'Kimmei', which is still quite rare. The leaves have yellow-white stripes and the culms are pale golden with green striae. Similar in vigour to f. *elegantissimus* but more vertical in habit.

Pleioblastus fortunei (syn. *P. variegatus*)
Dwarf Whitestripe Bamboo

Pointed and slightly curved leaves are dramatically striped white and cream on the short thin culms, forming dense colonies of spiky tufts. Usually seen as ground cover.

Culms: Maximum diameter 0.6 cm (0.25 in.)
Leaves: 12 × 1.25 cm (5 × 0.5 in.)

"Clean, fresh and colourful growth – will certainly impress."

Checklist

✗ Non-invasive

✓ **Short (0.3–1.5 m)**

✗ Medium (1.5–3.5 m)

✗ Tall (3.5 m +)

✓ **Cold hardy**

✓ **Heat tolerant**

✓ **Drought tolerant**

✗ Moisture tolerant

✓ **Pots and containers**

✓ **Good for plant association**

✓ **Waterside planting**

✓ **Hedging, screening and windbreaks**

→ The bright, fresh leaves of *Pleioblastus fortunei*

Hardiness and aspect

Min. −25°C (−13°F), zone 5
Sun or light shade

Dimensions

Height: 60 cm–1.5 m (2–5 ft.), average 90 cm (3 ft.)
Spread: 1–1.5 m (3.3–5 ft.) in 10 years

Uses and combinations

The possibilities of colour association are limitless, as this bamboo's shortness and vivid striping makes it useful in any scheme. Try it in the foreground of any dark colour. For shrubs, I suggest *Viburnum sargentii* 'Onondaga', with its rich, velvety purple foliage. For perennials, use *Crocosmia masoniorum*, with its beautiful late sprays of fiery orange-red flowers, held by the broad, sword-like pleated greenery. Also stunning and long-lived in pots.

This bamboo is mostly seen labelled as *Pleioblastus variegatus*. It was introduced by Robert Fortune from cultivation in Japan and because of this, the name *fortunei* is more widely recognized. A short, grassy bamboo, for best display of its undulating waves of spiky foliage it does need to form a reasonably sized colony. The rhizome is thin and shallow and can be easily chopped and pulled from the ground, should you need to control it. The new spring and summer growth is always the freshest and most colourful but a harsh winter may mark and stain the leaves, especially in pots. Once established, this bamboo can be sheared to the ground annually in late winter (or before new basal shoots are visible). Another good reason for this cropping is to keep its height in check – this bamboo always looks better at low level with the stark variegated leaves angled for viewing. If left without pruning, many of the thin culms become top heavy and may become arched and tangled. Although retaining reasonable colour in dark shade, the culms tend to draw upwards looking for light and flounder in all directions, so give it an open aspect for best effect.

I have grown this species with great effect in shallow pans, similar to those used by alpine plant enthusiasts. With annual pruning, regular soaking and lack of feed, the bamboo becomes stunted, creating a bright, miniature bonsai forest. Eventual division and repotting will be necessary, but five or six years of enjoyment is likely before that task.

← Plain green but fresh leaves of *Pleioblastus* 'Gauntlettii'

Look out for

Pleioblastus 'Gauntlettii' is considered a possible misnomer by many bamboo addicts, being suggested as identical to *Pleioblastus humilus* var. *pumilus*. My stock of 'Gauntlettii' always remains similar in structure to *Pleioblastus fortunei* and also relishes the hard annual pruning. To most gardeners the naming is not as important as the effect, but 'Gauntlettii' is a good choice if you require simple, green and robust.

Pleioblastus gramineus
Gramineus

Taller than most in the genus, with green, rounded culms and persistent papery sheaths. New culms begin to grow upright, but arch lightly in subsequent years with the weight of the high curved branches of long but narrow leaves, providing a willow-like effect. Can remain as a tight clump for many years before doing a runner.
Culms: Maximum diameter 2 cm (0.8 in.)
Leaves: 23 × 1.25 cm (9 × 0.5 in.)

Hardiness and aspect
Min. −20°C (−4°F), zone 6
Sun or shade

Dimensions
Height: 2–5 m (6.5–16.5 ft.), average 3 m (10 ft.)
Spread: 1–2 m (3.3–6.5 ft.) in 10 years

Uses and combinations
Arch it over a pond or allow it to form a fountain in the centre of a woodland clearing. Best of all, grow it

"A pleasing individual, unique in structure ..."

Checklist

✗ Non-invasive

✗ Short (0.3–1.5 m)

✓ **Medium (1.5 –3.5 m)**

✗ Tall (3.5 m +)

✓ **Cold hardy**

✓ **Heat tolerant**

✓ **Drought tolerant**

✗ Moisture tolerant

✗ Pots and containers

✓ **Good for plant association**

✓ **Waterside planting**

✗ Hedging, screening and windbreaks

→ The elegant, weeping structure on a young *Pleioblastus gramineus*

on either side of a path where it will shoot vertically by the edge but create a natural bamboo tunnel of foliage overhead.

Becoming more common in cultivation, this willowy and elegant bamboo has been referred to as looking like a "giant tree grass." Well, I couldn't describe it better myself. The specific name of *gramineus* does actually refer to the grass family of *gramineae*. Only native to the isolated Ryukyu Islands between Japan and Taiwan, this plant is tolerant of salt-laden winds and suited to a wide range of locations and uses. This is outstanding beside ponds, but beware of the shoots if your pond is butyl or clay lined. Put in a barrier of concrete edging or similar before planting to keep it at bay if required.

As a youngster it can be quite ragged, with shredded sheaths and damaged or starved leaves, but this is nearly always down to its confinement in nursery pots. In the garden, it is more lush and quickly develops into a pleasing individual, unique in its structure amongst the bamboos. The tall culms hold up a cascade of branches and long, slightly twisted leaves that wave in the breeze.

Look out for

Pleioblastus linearis was better known before its partial demise through flowering in the mid 1980s, but thankfully much seed was produced and the species is once more readily available. Nearly identical to *Pleioblastus gramineus* apart from its slightly hairy culm sheaths and flattened, long leaves, this is equally at home in sun or shade.

Pleioblastus chino var. *hisauchii* is native to China

→ Unusual sheath colouring on a developing culm of *Pleioblastus chino* var. *hisauchii*

and is well used in gardens and landscapes there. It is a distinctly woody variety, having tall culms that grow to between 3 m and 5 m (10–16.5 ft.) and mature quickly. The leaves are long and narrow but generally broader than the two species just mentioned. It also has dark culms with a white bloomy ring below the nodes.

Pleioblastus pygmaeus
Pygmy Bamboo

There is much variation as regards the leaves and size of this bamboo, but as a general rule, the smaller the leaves, the shorter the bamboo will be, although some forms can also be lax and ungainly. The tiny leaves are held rigidly on wispy culms, while in winter the leaves may be uniformly and attractively bleached at the tips.
Culms: Maximum diameter 0.3 cm (0.15 in.)
Leaves: 5 × 0.5 cm (2 × 0.2 in.). Small, in rows

Hardiness and aspect

Min. −29°C (−20°F), zone 4
Sun or light shade

Dimensions

Height: 20–60 cm (0.6–2 ft.), average 30 cm (1 ft.)
Spread: 1–4 m (3.3–13 ft.) in 10 years

Uses and combinations

Although less aggressive than its counterparts, the true clone is still capable of covering ground at a steady pace but is less likely to drain the soil of nutrients or water due to its tiny structure. This makes it ideal for cover amongst small trees, shrubs and other bamboos. Its darkness is useful when planting in drifts with other short bamboos, such as *Pleioblastus fortunei* and *Pleioblastus viridistriatus* to provide a vivid patchwork of colour. It can also be razed to the ground before spring to provide room for fresh new growth. Very likeable as a low, formal sectioning when contained and brilliant in pots where it is long-lived and rewarding. Cut it back late in winter to help keep up appearances.

In an effort to be precise about the description of this bamboo, because of its variables in the trade, I will stress the following points. If you buy from a specialist bamboo grower, you shouldn't have a problem in obtaining the correct plant, but just for comparison ask if you can compare it with *Pleioblastus pygmaeus*

> *"The tiniest of all the temperate bamboos."*

Checklist

✗ Non-invasive
✓ **Short (0.3–1.5 m)**
✗ Medium (1.5–3.5 m)
✗ Tall (3.5 m +)
✓ **Cold hardy**
✓ **Heat tolerant**
✓ **Drought tolerant**
✗ Moisture tolerant
✓ **Pots and containers**
✓ **Good for plant association**
✓ **Waterside planting**
✗ Hedging, screening and windbreaks

→ The tiny leaves of *Pleioblastus pygmaeus* (right) compared to the very large leaf of *Indocalamus hamadae*

'Distichus' (described later). At its maximum, the leaf area of the *pygmaeus* should be only twenty-five per cent of that of 'Distichus'. If you buy one from a chain store or supermarket, you could be taking a chance. Many plants supplied to these giant retailers are mass produced by wholesalers who have well controlled techniques to create plants of identical structure and quality. Dwarfing agents (usually chemical) are often applied to keep plants compact and appealing to customers, in readiness for impulse purchases. Two

years later, you may realise your mistake.

The true species has two parallel lines of leaves held horizontally from the central rib, usually with a single vertical leaf at the apex. In winter, the individual leaves can point slightly downwards as a reaction to the cold. Leaf bleaching is often seen in exposed or open aspects but this adds to the character. If you are fortunate enough to find the true species, you will be safe in the knowledge that you now own the tiniest of all temperate bamboos.

← The fan like leaf arrangement of *Pleioblastus pygmaeus* 'Distichus' is very distinct

Look out for

As mentioned earlier, *Pleioblastus pygmaeus* 'Distichus' is larger in leaf and structure, attaining some 1 m (3.3 ft.) in height on a rich soil. The freshest of green leaves point upwards from the culm tip at forty-five degree angles in a pronounced fan-like effect. This bamboo is very aggressive and not for the faint hearted, however it is reliable in pots.

Pleioblastus shibuyanus 'Tsuboi'
Tsuboi

One of the brightest and boldest bamboos, displaying elegant plumes of white striped leaves. Young plants often cover the culms completely in leaves and branches and are compact in habit. Older plants will usually be more open and aggressive, with well spaced culms and more height. The green culms with straw coloured sheathing will be visible below the leaf canopy.

Culms: Maximum diameter 1.25 cm (0.5 in.)
Leaves: 15 × 2 cm (6 × 0.8 in.). Narrow.

Hardiness and aspect

Min. −25°C (−13°F), zone 5
Sun or light shade

Dimensions

Height: 1–2.5 m (3.3–8.2 ft.), average 2 m (6.5 ft.)
Spread: 1 cm–4 m (3.3–14 ft.) in 10 years

Uses and combinations

Makes a good background for the timber bamboos and their bare, basal culm structure. Dark culms will show vividly against the bright variegation. This bamboo loves being clipped at the tops of the culms, where secondary branching then creates tufts of well spaced foliage along the culms, all very Japanese and arty. For all its vigour, this is surprisingly good in pots where it remains compact and colourful with little attention other than the need for water.

My opening gambit when discussing this bamboo with customers is usually betting them that they can't say its full name with a mouthful of rice. The resultant inflections and contortions of their facial muscles when attempting it always puts a smile on the face.

This bamboo is almost schizoid with its inconsistent habits in gardens – it never ceases to amaze me with its unpredictability. I have seen plants remain compact and clumping in gravel gardens, short and menacing in open woodland and then there is the plant in my garden. With many culms now exceeding 3 m (10 ft.) tall, it also covers ten or more strides across the ground. I have yet to see one taller and more dominant. It does a good job of filling the space between much taller bamboos and lighting up the glade between the taller dark greenery. Every year, I resolve to cut a winding path through the bamboo, removing any inferior culms in reach at the same time. If and when I find the time for such a task, it will be worth remembering that I will also

"The leaves are consistently bright in sun or half-shade."

Checklist

✗ Non-invasive

✗ Short (0.3–1.5 m)

✓ **Medium (1.5–3.5 m)**

✗ Tall (3.5 m +)

✓ **Cold hardy**

✓ **Heat tolerant**

✓ **Drought tolerant**

✗ Moisture tolerant

✓ **Pots and containers**

✓ **Good for plant association**

✓ **Waterside planting**

✓ **Hedging, screening and windbreaks**

→ The bright foliage of *Pleioblastus shibuyanus* 'Tsuboi' in shady woodland

have to prevent new culms emerging from the path annually. A simple kick when they emerge is enough to stop them in their tracks.

Slender culms appear in late spring, producing multiple branches at acute angles to the culms, so if you wish to prune to reduce height, do this just above the nodes where the branches appear and the cuts will be covered by the upward angled branches. The variegated leaves are consistently bright in sun or half-shade, but I recommend the latter, as it is much more effective.

Look out for

If you thrive on a challenge, try *Sinobambusa tootsik* 'Variegata'. Although from a different genus it is also brightly variegated. A medium height, vertical bamboo that is slow to mature, it loves being pruned and shaped into a pom-pom effect. The branches can be shortened and are naturally well spaced along the culms. This is revered in Japan for its tasteful quality is used frequently in plantings surrounding temples.

Pleioblastus viridistriatus (syn. *P. auricomus*)
Kamuro Bamboo

Instantly identifiable as the only temperate bamboo with a true yellow leaf colouring. A low, reed-like habit forms colonies of leafy thin culms, which are often purple tinted. Leaves are matte golden yellow with variable pale and dark green longitudinal striping.

Culms: Maximum diameter 1 cm (0.4 in.)
Leaves: 18 × 2.5 cm (7 × 1 in.)

Hardiness and aspect

Min. −25°C (−13°F), zone 5
Sun or half shade

Dimensions

Height: 1–1.8 m (3.3–6 ft.), average 1.2 m (4 ft.)
Spread: 1–2 m (3.3–6.5 ft.) in 10 years

Uses and combinations

As multipurpose as it gets, apart from the one basic need of good light, as in shade the bright golden colouring fades to a lacklustre lime-green. Use it in sweeping drifts by large ponds or as foreground planting to large shrubs and trees. In a mixed border, try it with the blue-flowered *Salvia* ×*sylvestris* 'Mainacht' in the foreground and the large, bamboo-like *Miscanthus sacchariflorus* erupting from the golden layer beneath. For autumn entertainment, a *Callicarpa bodinieri* 'Profusion', with its surprising display of bright purple fruits, will make your friends think that you are a professional garden designer. If pruned and trimmed regularly to promote fresh colourful growth, they will be successful in any pot.

Already widely cultivated in the United States and Europe, this is certainly a useful and bold garden plant, being one of the best yellow variegated plants

there is. This is also more suited to mixed border planting than some of the other short *Pleioblastus*, being less aggressive.

The foliage is at its best with rich-banana yellow colouring and vivid green striping from spring through to late summer. Early leaf growth can also have faint pink or purple tints and to accompany this, the green culms can also be stained purple. This effect is best seen on mature plants in good light. The surfaces of the leaves are covered in minute hairs, providing a rich, velvety appearance. As autumn and winter approach it will lose some of its appeal, as the colour fades in the decreasing sunlight and the cool nights can cause the leaves to hang forlornly. An established plant is best cropped to the ground each winter because as hardy as it is, this is really just a bamboo for warmer months. Its brief and exuberant display is more than enough to make it a garden worthy bamboo. If left unpruned, the culms will produce secondary shoots that will rise upwards to 1.8 m (6 ft.) or more and appear sparse and lanky. Keep it low to keep it lush.

In dry conditions, it benefits from the lightest of shade, losing a little colour but still looking fresh. It is most at home in moist cooler gardens, as here the height of the plant will become much shorter and the colour much bolder.

Look out for

Pleioblastus viridistriatus f. *chrysophyllus* has yellow leaves with no green striping. The toning ranges from lemon to a fresh lime-green, with a splash of chartreuse for good measure. Similar in height but less vigorous and said to burn in full sun, although it hasn't in my experience of it.

"Rich, banana-yellow colouring and vivid green striping."

Checklist

✗ Non-invasive

✓ **Short (0.3–1.5 m)**

✗ Medium (1.5–3.5 m)

✗ Tall (3.5 m +)

✓ **Cold hardy**

✓ **Heat tolerant**

✓ **Drought tolerant**

✗ Moisture tolerant

✓ **Pots and containers**

✓ **Good for plant association**

✓ **Waterside planting**

✗ Hedging, screening and windbreaks

→ *Pleioblastus viridistriatus* with fresh yellow variegated leaves

→ Lemon and lime colouring of *Pleioblastus viridistriatus* f. *chrysophyllus*

Pseudosasa japonica
Arrow Bamboo or Hardy Bamboo

This plant has the largest leaves for a bamboo of this size. Colonies of tightly packed culms can form different sized plantings according to location, but this is always imposing with its rigid structure. Rich, hanging green leaves from single branches off each node. It has persistent culm sheaths that are hairy when young and surround the dark green to yellow-green culms, giving a striped effect.

Culms: Maximum diameter 2 cm (0.8 in.)
Leaves: 30 × 3 cm (12 × 1.2 in.)

Hardiness and aspect

Min. −23°C (−10°F), zone 5–6
Sun or part shade

Dimensions

Height: 3–5 m (10–16.5 ft.), average 4 m (13 ft.)
Spread: 1–3 m (3.3–10 ft.) in 10 years

Uses and combinations

One of the best windbreaks and screens of any plant group, it is also tolerant of salt laden winds. Its potential aggressive behaviour also means it is suitable for stabilizing banks, especially by natural ponds and lakes, as it does not mind the changes in water level once it has established. It will keep well in pots for all its vigour if thinned of old culms regularly.

Already widely grown because it is tough, speedy and architectural, this bamboo has definitely been put through its paces. Native to Japan and South Korea and also widely naturalized in parts of China, this was an early introduction to the West. Alongside *Fargesia murielae*, this was much favoured by gardeners at the turn of the twentieth century and is still popular because of its hardiness and adaptability.

The sharp, pointed shoots emerge into tall and slender culms that are green at first and become pale with age. The single branches produced from the unobtrusive nodes can ramify in subsequent years, producing dense bunches of downward pointing leaves. Old culms can become congested and appear ragged with the flaking persistent sheathing. Frequent thinning and removal of sheathing will greatly enhance the bamboo's appearance. Another bonus is that these make excellent dried canes for use in the garden. Known as the arrow bamboo, it has indeed been used to make these weapons in Japan. Although the culms are thin walled, they are are strong with indistinct nodes, making them relatively smooth and straight.

Yet again, this bamboo's habit can vary from one extreme to the other. I have a vast colony in my garden that stands at 8 × 3 m (26 × 10 ft.) and gives me much privacy from a neighbouring garden. However, I know of another plant on similar soil that is probably a tenth of the size of my plant, but is twice as old. I drive past this compact specimen regularly and to my knowledge it has never been checked in its spread and is not contained by any barrier.

Look out for

Pseudosasa japonica 'Tsutsumiana' is quite short in stature, being at least half the average size of the species, but still has a strong, vertical and leafy appearance. The key feature is the swollen mature culms that are bulbous above the nodes, which also produces a slight spiralling or zigzag effect. To appreciate these swellings (it has to be done), I suggest removing low branches and all the persistent sheaths at the base of the plant regularly.

> *"Still popular because of its hardiness and adaptability."*

Checklist

✗ Non-invasive
✗ Short (0.3–1.5 m)
✗ Medium (1.5–3.5 m)
✓ Tall (3.5 m +)
✓ Cold hardy
✓ Heat tolerant
✓ Drought tolerant
✗ Moisture tolerant
✓ Pots and containers
✓ Good for plant association
✓ Waterside planting
✓ Hedging, screening and windbreaks

→ *Pseudosasa japonica* in a very exposed aspect

Pseudosasa japonica 'Akebonosuji' is a variegated form. Leaves are variable as some are almost pure white and some plain green while others are striped cream and silver.

→ *Pseudosasa japonica* 'Tsutsumiana' grows well in pots

Sasa kurilensis 'Shimofuri'
Frosty Bamboo or Shimofuri

This plant's large, hanging leaves have very fine white and green linear striping when viewed closely, but appear silvery from a distance. Slender, medium height culms are produced early and emerge yellow with a white ring below each node, after which they quickly turn green but ripen to a yellow-green colour after a year or two. The early sheathing protecting the culms is unmistakable with its green and yellow colouring that is edged with deep plum-violet.

Culms: Maximum diameter 2 cm (0.8 in.)
Leaves: 30 × 3 cm (12 × 1.2 in.)

Hardiness and aspect
Min. −30°C (−22°F), zone 4
Sun or shade

Dimensions
Height: 2–3 m (6.5–10 ft.), average 2.5 m (8.2 ft.)
Spread: 1–4 m (3.3–13 ft.) in 10 years

Uses and combinations
Stunning with anything red, I have a large coral bark maple, *Acer palmatum* 'Senkaki' (syn. 'Sango-kaku') erupting proudly from this plant's foliage canopy. The red branches almost glow from the silvery foliage beneath. If thinned of old culms regularly, this bamboo can be successfully underplanted. My plant is at the edge of a path and at the base of the bamboo I have Christmas box, *Sarcococca hookeriana* var. *digyna* 'Purple Stem' with its rich winter scent, the green flowered *Helleborus foetidus* and evergreen *Epimedium*. All are tolerant of the competition and shade from above.

The *kurilensis* species and its forms inhabit some of the most extreme temperatures. Originating from the Kuril and Sakhalin Islands off the eastern seaboard of Russia and north of Japan. In these areas they show belittlement from their harsh origins. We are fortunately more blessed in our more temperate gardens and can therefore obtain the best from this bamboo.

'Shimofuri' is uniquely variegated with faint, white margined leaves and brush-stroked white striping. From the beginnings of the new, colourful shoots of yellow, green and violet-red, the culms are quick to mature, reaching their full height by early summer and flamboyantly opening their leaves to catch the warmth of the sun. As I sit here in the murk of January after a harder winter than usual, I can see my 'Shimofuri' through the study window – it glows enticingly in the gloom. The leaves have all tip bleached uniformly as a result of the cold, an attractive feature in its own right.

This bamboo can be a monster, so allow it some room. A mature plant can have all the previous year's culms removed, but only after the new have fully developed in mid-summer. This helps to slow the bamboo down and stop it from becoming congested. It also gets rid of any bleached foliage from the previous winter, thus keeping it fresh in appearance. Alternatively, new secondary branches and leaves will form on old culms, allowing for the removal of the old leaves and branches should you wish for a denser colony. My plant seems happy in full sun, although the soil is moist which is beneficial for this plant as the leaves may curl if too dry. Plants I have seen elsewhere have been grown in part shade where it performs just as well, although it is tolerant of drier soils. It is not recommended for hotter and drier regions – as the leaves curl inwards they will scorch in

> *"Faintly white margined leaves and brush-stroked white striping."*

Checklist

✗ Non-invasive

✗ Short (0.3–1.5 m)

✓ **Medium (1.5–3.5 m)**

✗ Tall (3.5 m+)

✓ **Cold hardy**

✗ Heat tolerant

✓ **Drought tolerant**

✗ Moisture tolerant

✓ **Pots and containers**

✓ **Good for plant association**

✓ **Waterside planting**

✓ **Hedging, screening and windbreaks**

→ The finely striped leaves of *Sasa kurilensis* 'Shimofuri'

the heat and the bamboo will generally be weak and lax in habit.

Look out for

Sasa kurilensis (the species) is taller with even larger leaves. It is best used as a large foliar feature in open woodland. *Sasa kurilensis* – short, is much more compact than either the species or 'Shimofuri' and makes a fine ground cover plant. The flattened sprays of large palmate leaves are always dark, fresh and

→ The palmate leaf arrangement of *Sasa kurilensis* – short

shiny. It rarely exceeds 1 m (3 ft.), making it a wonderful container plant.

Sasa palmata f. *nebulosa*
Palmate Bamboo, Nebulosa

Medium height spreader with enormous, tropical looking leaves and unusual dark brown-black blotches on older culms. Some winter leaf bleaching can occur in harsh weather, but otherwise it appears fresh and unscathed. It advances quickly and points its leaves outwards from the culm, as it reaches out for more room.

Culms: Maximum diameter 1.25 cm (0.5 in.)
Leaves: 30 × 10 cm (12 × 4 in.)

Hardiness and aspect

Min. −30° C (−22°F), zone 4
Sun or shade

Dimensions

Height: 1.5–3 m (5–10 ft.), average 2 m (6.5 ft.)
Spread: 1.5–6 m (5–20 ft.) in 10 years

Uses and combinations

For association in the normal garden, forget it, unless you've got something to pair it with on a truly grand scale. It will rampage through anything in its way like an army on the march. It is, however, essential for the tropical look, so either keep it in check very regularly, or grow it in the confines of a large tub or raised bed. In pots, it complements the short and grassy variegated bamboos or other bold architectural plants. Use it with the grassy *Restio* from South Africa with the layered compact form of *Pinus parviflora* for a contemporary look. If it is to be grown in pots, then old culms must be removed regularly after new ones have emerged. This stops the container becoming top heavy and falling over in the wind.

This plant is "Possibly the number one reason for potential divorce," I frequently joke with customers, as my plant of this *Sasa* has almost entirely engulfed the washing line, as my wife frequently reminds me. As the bamboo is heading out towards the garden boundary, I am still secretly hoping that one year it will reach the neighbouring field and mingle with the sugar beet. For all its beauty, this bamboo is probably partly responsible for the bad press that bamboos often receive. As one of the earliest and most widespread introductions, it was often wrongly placed in areas too small for its needs.

A single rhizome from a mature plant can creep many metres under the soil in just one year, not forgetting the numerous pointed buds that (if our puppy does not feast on them) will shoot upwards into culms the following year. If you don't have the room then confine it to bounds. In the garden it prefers a cool moist soil, while in dry, arid soils with the sun overhead the leaves will curl and can parch at the edges. In pots, give it some shade by a wall or under trees in the hottest of summers.

I once had the luxury (or chore) of removing this *Sasa* from a friend's garden. It was only 1 m (3.3 ft.) across at the base with a few probing rhizomes beginning to move outwards. It had been buried in a large tub within the soil, in the hope it would be contained. Not so with this bamboo. Unseen, the rhizomes had snuck over the edge of the pot and had also emerged from the drainage holes beneath. On the upside, my acquisition did make a fine exhibition specimen after the two hours of hard exertion spent removing it.

Look out for

Sasa oshidensis doesn't have the same tropical appeal, but it is more tolerant of heat and drier conditions

"*Its speedy outward development could be likened to a Triffid.*"

Checklist

✗ Non-invasive
✗ Short (0.3–1.5 m)
✓ **Medium (1.5–3.5 m)**
✗ Tall (3.5 m +)
✓ **Cold hardy**
✗ Heat tolerant
✓ **Drought tolerant**
✗ Moisture tolerant
✓ **Pots and containers**
✓ **Good for plant association**
✓ **Waterside planting**
✓ **Hedging, screening and windbreaks**

→ *Sasa palmata* f. *nebulosa* marching outwards from the main clump

and is similar in height. *Sasa tsuboiana* is variable in habit with smaller leaves. I have seen it grow in a tight clump as well as spreading far and wide. It has a lush and shiny appearance and is tolerant of exposure.

→ A *Sasa* leaf's shadow against the sunlight

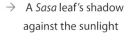

Checklist

X Non-invasive

✓ **Short (0.3–1.5 m)**

X Medium (1.5–3.5 m)

X Tall (3.5 m +)

✓ **Cold hardy**

✓ **Heat tolerant**

✓ **Drought tolerant**

✓ **Moisture tolerant**

✓ **Pots and containers**

✓ **Good for plant association**

✓ **Waterside planting**

✓ **Hedging, screening and windbreaks**

← *Sasa veitchii* by the side of a woodland track

Sasa veitchii
Kuma Grass Bamboo

The creamy, bleached leaf margins on this low and wide spreading bamboo make it unmistakable in the winter months. Fresh, ovate dark leaves in summer are held by plum-tinted culms when grown in full sun.

Culms: Maximum diameter 0.6 cm (0.25 in.)

Leaves: 25 × 6 cm (10 × 0.25 ft.)

Hardiness and aspect
Min. −25°c (−13°F), zone 5
Sun or shade

Dimensions
Height: 1–1.5 m (3.3–5 ft.), average 1.2 m (4 ft.)
Spread: 1–4 m (3.3–13 ft.) in 10 years

Uses and combinations

This plant's mat of searching rhizomes makes this ideal for stabilizing banks, slopes or eroded areas. In large pots, it is an attractive winter feature, particularly when the leaves are frosted. Wherever it is used, allow for a generous planting as it looks better en masse – small plants in pots can look battered and bruised by the end of a winter. The creamy bleaching and dark centres to the leaves are most effective in the winter garden with pollarded willows growing through the cover. Try the orange stemmed *Salix ×rubens* 'Basfordiana' or the ghostly silver of *Salix acutifolia*.

Although not a variegated bamboo, the attractive and crisp winter leaf bleaching does often fool people into believing it actually is. Recently, I received an email from a local villager who was enquiring on behalf of friends about a bamboo they had seen in a garden. The description was as follows: "They saw a clump of bamboo growing around the base of an oak tree. It was 2.5–3 ft. tall (less than 1 m) and green at the centre of the leaf, with thick, creamy-yellow bands around the leaf margins." After racking my brains as to which of the few variegated bamboos this description could be, I started to froth at the mouth as I anticipated unveiling a newly discovered form. However, sanity quickly returned and I soon realised that the plant in question was *Sasa veitchii*. I replied and sent through a photograph of the leaves and this was confirmed as the correct plant.

This is an important landscape bamboo that forms the boldest of plantings, with the winter leaf bleaching offering a quality that no other plant is capable of. However, once established this is best cropped in early spring, which will keep it short, tidy and uniform. It is equally at home in an open, exposed aspect or in a sheltered woodland area, making it tolerant of both moist and dry soils.

← The shorter habit of *Sasa quelpaertensis*

Look out for

Sasa quelpaertensis has the closest resemblance to *veitchii*, with similar pseudo-variegation of the leaves. It is usually shorter, equally aggressive and also benefits from an annual shearing.

Sasaella ramosa
Ramosa Bamboo

Usually seen as huge green tracts in woodland gardens of old, this is aggressive unless contained. Although short in height, the thin but strong grass-like culms hold the palmate fans of leaves impressively. The leaves, often bleached at the edges can wither and hang loosely in the winter – the effect is not displeasing when seen in large areas of planting.

Culms: Maximum diameter 0.6 cm (0.25 in.)
Leaves: 15 × 2 cm (6 × 0.8 in.)

Checklist

✗ Non-invasive

✓ **Short (0.3–1.5 m)**

✗ Medium (1.5–3.5 m)

✗ Tall (3.5 m +)

✓ **Cold hardy**

✓ **Heat tolerant**

✗ Drought tolerant

✓ **Moisture tolerant**

✓ **Pots and containers**

✓ **Good for plant association**

✓ **Waterside planting**

✓ **Hedging, screening and windbreaks**

← *Sasaella ramosa* used successfully as underplanting beneath taller plants

Hardiness and aspect

Min. −30°C (−22°F), zone 4

Sun or shade

Dimensions

Height: 60 cm–2 m (2–6.5 ft.), average 1 m (3.3 ft.)

Spread: 2–6 m (6.5–20 ft.) in 10 years

Uses and combinations

Useful for edging or as a basal plant in raised beds or restricted borders. It is not a greedy bamboo as it will allow taller, woody plants to grow with it in harmony. It also likes to be let loose to form huge billowing colonies, but only do so if you are blessed with the necessary space.

This short bamboo has long been cultivated in the West as it has been widely recognized for its ground covering ability. The short, slender culms are plain green, ripening to a much paler shade. As the culms are produced in close proximity to each other, the developing branches interlock to hold the colony upright. A young nursery plant without this mass of self-supporting structure will always look floppy and lifeless.

This bamboo does prefer a moist soil and can look jaded when too dry, in confined spaces some additional summer irrigation will prove beneficial. In winter, the leaves can often hang and bleach as a form of shelter from the cold. The best specimens I have ever seen of this plant have been annually mowed to the ground before spring shooting time. The plant's rhizomes are strong, plentiful and well able to cope with this slaughter. In the wilds of east Asia, this bamboo is normally razed to the ground by deep snowfall or bitter cold. As a result, it has developed the ability to regenerate strongly.

Happy in deep shade, this plant prevents the erosion of slopes and natural pond edging, makes a fine weed suppressant and is easy to maintain, needing only an annual shearing.

← The many different tone of cream and green on leaves of *Sasaella masamuneana* 'Albostriata'

Look out for

Sasaella masamuneana is of a similar structure, but is taller with longer leaves. Noted for its deep purple culm colouring in an open aspect, this species has two variegated offspring, *Sasaella masamuneana* f. *aureostriata*, which is quite rare and develops longitudinal mustard-yellow leaf striping and *Sasaella masamuneana* 'Aureostriata', which is already a popular short form for containers and brightly variegated in summer with creamy-white striping. This form is not as vigorous as the other *Sasaella*, making it much more useful for the smaller garden. It benefits from annual thinning of old culms and branches as the new develop from late spring onwards. Only very well established plants are able to endure the hard cropping needed for the other forms.

Semiarundinaria fastuosa
Temple Bamboo, Noble Bamboo

Tall, stately and steadfastly vertical with short upward pointing branches on mature culms. The new culms are rich green and become mottled and stained with burgundy and bronze tones after two or three years. This plant has distinctive culm sheathing that is pale green at first but quickly turns to a pink-silver with iridescent pale purple on the inside. It is clumping at first but also has the ability to form good sized colonies.

Culms: Maximum diameter 4 cm (1.6 in.)

Leaves: 15 × 4 cm (6 × 1.6 in.)

Hardiness and aspect
Min. −25°C (−13°F), zone 5
Full sun

Dimensions
Height: 6–10 m (20–33 ft.), average 7 m (23 ft.)
Spread: 1–3 m (3.3–10 ft.) in 10 years

Checklist

✗ Non-invasive
✗ Short (0.3–1.5 m)
✗ Medium (1.5–3.5 m)
✓ **Tall (3.5 m +)**
✓ **Cold hardy**
✓ **Heat tolerant**
✓ **Drought tolerant**
✗ Moisture tolerant
✓ **Pots and containers**
✓ **Good for plant association**
✓ **Waterside planting**
✓ **Hedging, screening and windbreaks**

← The stout, vertical structure of *Semiarundinaria fastuosa*

Uses and combinations

Already a tried and tested windbreak and screen, this plant is also tolerant of salty air in coastal regions. Because of its unwavering vertical structure, it is excellent in confined borders as long as the rhizome is checked regularly or restricted by edging. It is much less invasive in cool regions. As an architectural plant, it emphasises any other nearby vertical structure.

Sometimes named the noble bamboo, this uniquely shaped plant is native to Japan. A bamboo of great character, it is the most impressive and tallest in the genus. Able to tolerate confinement, it will certainly need some restriction in warm locations, where it is normally aggressive.

Lush green culms emerge from the late spring shoots, covered in pale green sheathing. As the culms expand upwards, the sheaths remain attached for a time but eventually turn creamy-silver or flushed pink. When the culms attain their full height, the sheaths loosen their grip and begin to angle away from the culms, hinging delicately from the centre of the sheath base. The purple, shiny, inner surface of the sheaths become visible and this is a memorable sight. The shedding process takes about a month. Old culms eventually lose their shine but they create a patchwork of blotches and staining with subtle burgundy tinting. Leaves are held close to the tops of the culms by the short, upward angled branches, so a specimen with well spaced culms will appear like a series of narrow, vertical columns.

Although generally quite refined (I have seen more clumps than large groves), it can randomly travel across the soil in dead-straight lines with incredible accuracy. In cool gardens, it will still grow respectably tall, if given time.

Look out for

Semiarundinaria fastuosa var. *viridis* is said to be taller and more invasive than the species. Green in all its

← *Semiarundinaria kagamiana*

parts, the old culms also do not colour like those of the species. However, my plant has remained shorter but has grown at a right angle from the original planting. Planted under the eaves of a large pine, it has moved out from under the shade and dry soil and into the open.

Semiarundinaria kagamiana does not have the overall height of *fastuosa*, but it is still rigid in structure and well suited to exposure. A classic Japanese style bamboo, it has the short branches of spreading fingered leaves. Thin it regularly to allow it light and the culms will reward you with their developing tones of rich burgundy-purple.

Semiarundinaria yashadake f. *kimmei*
Kimmei Bamboo

This is the shortest bamboo to have reliably golden culms, but is completely different in appearance to the golden *Phyllostachys*. The culms are slender with thick alternate green striping on the internodes, while the sparse fresh green foliage has occasional thin, creamy striping. Its high branching means the stark golden culms are always visible. This bamboo can remain as a tight clump or form short runs of culms, radiating outwards from the original planting. However, it is rarely a nuisance. It is V-shaped when young but becomes stronger and more vertical with maturity.
Culms: Maximum diameter 4 cm (1.6 in.)
Leaves: 14 × 1.25 cm (5.5 × 0.5 in.)

Hardiness and aspect
Min. −22°c (−8°F), zone 6
Sun or part shade

Dimensions
Height: 3–7.5 m (10–24.6 ft.), average 4 m (13 ft.)
Spread: 1–2.5 m (3.3–8.2 ft.) in 10 years

Uses and combinations
Because of its slender stature and short height, this is a useful border plant that flirts with (rather than dominates) its neighbours. Mix with a lower, large leaved bamboo such as *Indocalamus tessellatus*. I have

"Its well mannered qualities and lightness allow for underplanting."

Checklist

✗ Non-invasive

✗ Short (0.3–1.5 m)

✗ Medium (1.5–3.5 m)

✓ Tall (3.5 m +)

✓ Cold hardy

✓ Heat tolerant

✓ Drought tolerant

✗ Moisture tolerant

✓ Pots and containers

✓ Good for plant association

✓ Waterside planting

✓ Hedging, screening and windbreaks

← Thin, deep golden culms on *Semiarundinaria yashadake* f. *kimmei*

seen it grow well in pots, where the culms have been selectively shortened so as to avoid a flat-topped look, forcing the development of lower branches that can also be shortened in a tufted fashion. The branches angle upwards, eventually covering up any cuts made to the tops of the culms. A delightful bamboo that gets better with age.

Young nursery plants can look sparse and dishevelled, but they quickly relish the luxury of being given more room, either in the ground or larger pots. New culms appear early in the summer, emerging yellow into sunlight and often tanning a deep pink-red in the first season on the side facing the sun. Add the quite thick green striping in comparison to the culm size, the gold backs to the new culms and you will be smitten at this point. On old culms, the yellow turns to a deep russet-gold and the green striping becomes paler, offering a good background to the paler new growth. It must be noted that the thin individual culms have a shorter life expectancy than those of the giant timber bamboos, so with this plant regular removal of old culms will be required. It demands no more than a minute or two of your annual attention to create a possible work of art, so this should not be a chore.

This bamboo is always easy to recommend, as I am often asked for a bamboo with golden culms that is manageable and not too tall or dominant. *Kimmei* is the only choice I am left with, being the only bamboo that matches these criteria. I have seen it in woodland glades where it provides a beacon-like effect, highlighting the surrounding gloom. In mixed borders, its well mannered qualities and lightness allow for underplanting with just about anything. It is also well suited to retained narrow borders or raised beds, as the confining of the roots will mean culms grow closer together than in open soil, with the density of top growth becoming suitable for trimming. Do not be put off by its early appearance of being top heavy, as once it finds its feet it will perform adequately in its new home.

Look out for
Semiarundinaria yashadake 'Gimmei', which has a reverse colouring of green culms with yellow striping and is a recent introduction. *Semiarundinaria makinoi* is small for the genus at 2 m (6.5 ft.), but has good spacing between the sturdy, thin culms and a well spaced, elegant framework of branches. This is an excellent choice for pots, being long-lived and easy to fuss over as it relishes attention.

Shibataea kumasasa
Ruscus Leaved Bamboo

Unlike any other bamboo with a squat and compact growth habit, this plant also has characteristic short yet broad leaves on almost non-existent branching. Distinctly shaped leaves have a spiky appearance, first opening very dark, then paling towards the end of the summer, and bleaching uniformly and attractively at the tips in winter. The upper parts of the thin culms have a slightly zigzag formation.
Culms: Maximum diameter 0.6 cm (0.25 in.)
Leaves: 7 × 2 cm (2.75 × 0.8 in.)

Hardiness and aspect
Min. −25°C (−13°F), zone 5
Light or half shade

Dimensions
Height: 75 cm–2 m (2.5–6.5 ft.), average 1 m (3.3 ft.)

Spread: 75 cm–1.2 m (2.5–5 ft.) in 10 years

Uses and combinations
Being miniature compared to most other bamboos, this should never be crowded. Use it at a border edge or in a refined more formal planting scheme or rock garden. In China and Japan, it is used extensively for low, clipped hedging and small ground cover areas. It does prefer a slightly acid soil, so if you can't use it in the garden it also does well in pots. Make sure you use ericaceous compost and collected rainwater for irrigation.

Rather strangely, this dwarf bamboo is allied to the much bigger *Phyllostachys* group. The grouping refers to the fact that the culms of *Shibataea* also have similar indented sulci to others in this group, although you would need a magnifying glass to see

Checklist

✓ **Non-invasive**

✓ **Short (0.3–1.5 m)**

✗ Medium (1.5– 3.5 m)

✗ Tall (3.5 m +)

✓ **Cold hardy**

✓ **Heat tolerant**

✓ **Drought tolerant**

✗ Moisture tolerant

✓ **Pots and containers**

✓ **Good for plant association**

✓ **Waterside planting**

✗ Hedging, screening and windbreaks

← A carefully thinned plant of *Shibataea kumasasa* is well suited to growing in pots

them. With the sulci present, the new culms are flattened and form a triangular cross-section that creates a slight zigzag at the top of each thin culm.

Once this bamboo is established, it is suited to light trimming to create low domes, mounds or formal edging and partitions. If left untrimmed, the beautiful leaf tip bleaching in the winter will become more evident. In the second year, this bleaching can start to look untidy as new growth will emerge through from the base. I always prefer to selectively remove all the previous year's growth carefully during mid-summer, for a display of new fresh greenery. If done annually, the plant will naturally stay lower. I have seen specimens that were left untouched for many years, which became so congested with impenetrable top growth that they became woody at the base and started to die-back.

If you are looking for a dwarf and tidy bamboo, but don't want the wandering habit of a *Pleioblastus*, then this would be the wisest choice.

leaves, growing slightly taller than *kumasasa*. It lends
itself well to clipping and shaping.

Thamnocalamus crassinodus 'Kew Beauty'
Kew Beauty Bamboo

Its powdery blue, thick culms emerge from pale
sheathing and their colour will last well into the
second season. The dark red tinted high branches
hold a froth of tiny leaves. Upright, with a slight arch
at the very top and resolutely clumping.
Culms: Maximum diameter 2 cm (0.8 in.)
Leaves: 6 × 0.5 cm (2.4 × 0.2 in.). Very small

Hardiness and aspect
Min. −15°c (5°f), zone 7
Light shade

Dimensions
Height: 3.5–5.5 m (11.5–18 ft.), average 4 m (13 ft.)
Spread: 75 cm–1.5 m (2.5–5 ft.) in 10 years

Uses and combinations
This is a useful mixed border plant, as anything
growing in the background can be seen appearing
through the plant's culms and foliage. The blue culm
colouring shows itself best with a dark background. I
have *Lonicera pileata* at a low level near it, with its fresh
layers of evergreen leaves. Weeping on one side, the
flexible branches of the evergreen *Cotoneaster serotinus*
with its red winter fruits flicker casually in the breeze.

The only drawback with this bamboo and
its relatives is their intolerance of high heat and
drought, as it is only suited to a cool temperate
climate. If you are fortunate enough to live in the
right place for this plant, then you are able to grow a

true beauty. New culms are a pale sky-blue, emerging
from tightly packed hairy sheaths at ground level. As
the new culms expand, the powder-blue internodes
become visible and the sheathing can briefly be
tinted purple before turning to parchment. Some
of the sheaths can persist into the winter months,
especially if they are protecting culms that emerged
late. An individual culm from a mature plant will
take only five or six weeks to reach its full height
before producing its complement of branches and
leaves. The foliage is held on the upper two thirds
of the plant and as the branches ripen, a dark red
toning becomes visible (old culms can also turn
dark purple-red). This blue and garnet-red colour
combination is unique to this cultivar and allows for
easy identification.

This and the others in the species are best placed
in light shade where sunlight can filter through and
highlight the stunning culm colour. Although the
rhizome is thick and the roots are fleshy, it does
react quickly to drought, something I have learned
to my cost. Even well established plants require
supplementary watering in the driest of times. My
'Kew Beauty' is planted under the loose canopies of
a silver willow, *Salix alba* var. *sericea*, a purple leaved
birch and the golden *Robinia pseudoacacia* 'Frisia', all of
which are older than the bamboo. Three years ago,
a combination of spring drought, short mid-summer
cloudbursts and then a dry end to the summer
stressed this bamboo to the point of near death.

Checklist

✓ **Non-invasive**

✗ Short (0.3–1.5 m)

✗ Medium (1.5–3.5 m)

✓ **Tall (3.5 m+)**

✓ **Cold hardy**

✗ Heat tolerant

✗ Drought tolerant

✓ **Moisture tolerant**

✓ **Pots and containers**

✓ **Good for plant association**

✓ **Waterside planting**

✗ Hedging, screening and windbreaks

← A new culm of *Thamnocalamus crassinodus* 'Kew Beauty' in all its glory

Two sets of shoots were produced early and late, but neither was able to fully develop due to the lack of moisture available at the time and most collapsed into a mushy mess. The mid-summer dousing came too late for the first crop of shoots and the second batch failed to mature, as their production occurred too late in the year. Many of the older culms died out in the autumn. The bamboo slowly recovered after two or three years, but in the interim it returned to its juvenile state and needed lots of tender loving care.

This is the worst that can happen, so hopefully you will not make the same mistake.

Look out for

Thamnocalamus crassinodus 'Merlyn' is of similar habit to 'Kew Beauty', with new blue culms. As well as the branches, these age to a yellow-green and do not have the redness of the latter plant. 'Merlyn' is also more vertical in habit and has slightly smaller leaves. *Thamnocalamus crassinodus* 'Gosainkund' provides paler,

← New dark shoots of 'Kew Beauty'

silvery grey-blue new culms, which are heavily sheathed. The branches and leaves are

→ *Thamnocalamus crassinodus* 'Merlyn'

much longer than on the other cultivars, creating an arching habit.

Thamnocalamus crassinodus 'Lang Tang'
Lang Tang Bamboo

This has the smallest leaves of any temperate bamboo, which are held on a very dense branch system that creates layers of fresh greenery above the bare culms. The new culms are blue and quite thick for their height, supporting a flattish-topped canopy above them.

Culms: Maximum diameter 2 cm (0.8 in.)
Leaves: 6 × 0.5 cm (2.4 × 0.2 in.). Very small

Hardiness and aspect
Min. −15°C (5°F), zone 7
Light shade

Dimensions
Height: 2.5–4.5 m (8.2–14.8 ft.), average 3.5 m (11.5 ft.)
Spread: 75 cm–1 m (2.5–3.3 ft.) in 10 years

Uses and combinations
By a path, this will eventually form an overhanging natural arch. Culms can be appreciated close up and the filigree foliage can be admired from below. Against a shady wall, it will erupt outwards, highlighting the layers of greenery against the solid background. The tiniest of leaves associate well with anything big, bold and large – my specimen of *Viburnum* ×*pragense* acts as a background for my plant, with its dark and shiny leaves. On the opposite side of the path, the large and variegated ×*Hibanobambusa tranquillans* 'Shiroshima' creates the other part of a walk through a bamboo tunnel.

A mature 'Lang Tang' is certainly a sight to behold. Always slightly shorter than the other cultivars, the culms are nevertheless equally as thick, although they look bolder with their stumpy, short internodes. The mass of tiny leaves create a cascading froth of tumbling pale greenery from dense branching at the ends of the culms. A young nursery plant will rarely show any thick structure or blue culms and is usually short, grassy and pale in leaf. It much prefers the open soil to being grown in pots. In the first few winters, young plants can desiccate in the cold, with the tiny leaves often closing up for protection. Wrap the plant lightly in a breathable netting or fleece or put up with it, knowing full well that it will recover quickly in the spring. As the bamboo becomes more established, it will become stronger and more able to cope with harsh conditions.

It is always difficult to choose between viewing this

Checklist

✓ **Non-invasive**

✗ Short (0.3–1.5 m)

✓ **Medium (1.5–3.5 m)**

✗ Tall (3.5 m +)

✓ **Cold hardy**

✗ Heat tolerant

✗ Drought tolerant

✓ **Moisture tolerant**

✗ Pots and containers

✓ **Good for plant association**

✓ **Waterside planting**

✗ Hedging, screening and windbreaks

← *Thamnocalamus crassinodus* 'Lang Tang' arching outwards over a path

bamboo from afar for its unique mushroom habit or close up for the stunning culm colouring, so it is a worthy addition to your collection.

Look out for

Thamnocalamus crassinodus – dwarf form, as yet with no name. This forms a low mop of arching greenery to an average of 2 m (6.5 ft.), displaying long and narrow leaves. The culms are totally obscured by

→ Pale sky-blue culms of 'Lang Tang'

the foliage and are a pale blue-green, so if you wish to view them carefully prune the arching tips.

> *"Always noted for its glossy, healthy appearance."*

Checklist

✓ **Non-invasive**

✗ Short (0.3–1.5 m)

✗ Medium (1.5–3.5 m)

✓ **Tall (3.5 m +)**

✓ **Cold hardy**

✓ **Heat tolerant**

✗ Drought tolerant

✓ **Moisture tolerant**

✓ **Pots and containers**

✓ **Good for plant association**

✓ **Waterside planting**

✓ **Hedging, screening and windbreaks**

→ A young hedge of the fresh green *Yushania anceps*

Yushania anceps
Jaunsar Bamboo

Depending on the aspect and growing conditions, this will be variable in height and form. Tall plants are a fresh green with dramatic arches of foliage at the top of the culms. Smaller plants will be more vertical, with less of the weeping habit. New green culms have a pale, powdery coating that is lost after the first season, in later years turning a glossy, pale yellow green.

Culms: Maximum diameter 2 cm (0.8 in.)

Leaves: 13 × 1.25 cm (5 × 0.5 in.)

Hardiness and aspect

Min. −18°C (0°F), zone 6

Sun or light shade

Dimensions

Height: 3–5 m (10–16.5 ft.), average 4 m (13 ft.)

Spread: 1–3 m (3.3–10 ft.) in 10 years

Uses and combinations

Makes a dramatic hedge or backdrop with its flowing layers of glossy foliage. Ideal for hedging or dark woodland areas where its lightness and form can be appreciated.

Respectfully hardy, this bamboo is native to India where it grows at very high altitudes near the Himalayas. In these remote locations, it is widely valued for animal fodder and household crafts such as basket making and matting. Technically this is a clump forming bamboo, but because of its vigour and keenness to grow, be very careful with it in smaller gardens. *Yushania* species have a distinct, tillering rhizome structure, meaning that new culms can develop from buds at the very base of existing culms. This provides the genus with a unique structural appearance of well spaced clusters of tightly packed culms.

Having flowered in cultivation a few times during the last century, there is now a mixture of original and (unnamed) variation seedlings, as not all plants suffered from flowering. The former are widely distributed in botanical gardens and large estates, as this was an early and fashionable introduction to their landscaping. Although perhaps not as widely planted in modern times due to its size, *anceps* is however still noted for its glossy, healthy appearance and mature characteristics. It can defoliate slightly during tough winter conditions as a result of its conditioning in the high altitudes of the wild. Leaves may also curl slightly in high heat. None of this is really detrimental to the plant, as it has the strength to recover quickly.

Look out for

Yushania anceps 'Pitt White' is highly sought after. It regenerated after a specific form flowered in the famous Pitt White garden in Devon, England. It is taller and has smaller leaves and old culms, which develop a rich purple-brown colouring. The slender culms can arch spectacularly towards the ground for a lofty 8 m (26 ft.) or more.

Yushania maculata
Tung Chuan 4

An unmistakable vertical bamboo, with new blue-grey culms, contrasting dark purple-brown sheathing and white bloom below the nodes. Older culms are dark green with paler, persistent sheathing. Leaves are a deep shining green, tapering to fine points with a finger-like effect.

Culms: Maximum diameter 1.5 cm (0.6 in.)

Leaves: 13 × 1.25 cm (5 × 0.5 in.). Narrow and willowy

Hardiness and aspect

Min. −18°C (0°F), zone 6

Sun or light shade

"One of the freshest wind tolerant bamboos there is."

Checklist

✗ Non-invasive
✗ Short (0.3–1.5 m)
✓ **Medium (1.5–3.5 m)**
✗ Tall (3.5 m +)
✓ **Cold hardy**
✓ **Heat tolerant**
✓ **Drought tolerant**
✗ Moisture tolerant
✓ **Pots and containers**
✓ **Good for plant association**
✓ **Waterside planting**
✓ **Hedging, screening and windbreaks**

→ A colourful new culm of *Yushania maculata*

Dimensions

Height: 3–5 m (10–16.5 ft.), average 3.5 m (11.5 ft.)
Spread: 1–2.5 m (3.3–8.2 ft.) in 10 years

Uses and combinations

This is an essential addition to any medium or large sized garden. It is always unscathed in any temperate environment, being drought and wind tolerant. If you haven't got the room for it, I have seen it grown successfully in large pots where the culms can be admired at close proximity. Pruning above the nodes to reduce height and aid stability in this situation is possible, as the upward pointing branches will help cover the cuts. For foreground planting, use something low and pale, such as snowdrops or the low white *Geranium sanguineum* 'Album', which will show up well with the darkness of the bamboo behind.

I have to confess this is one of my favourite bamboos and is also spoken of highly by other authors. Reading through a few descriptions, I note the words 'outstanding', 'striking' and 'superb' and I have to say that I couldn't agree more. Much hardier than was first thought, this has proved to be one of the freshest, most wind tolerant bamboos there is. Every part of this bamboo is striking at some time or another. In mid summer, the new culms have wonderfully coloured sheathing that is not easily described, as they vary from a rich red-purple to a rusty, dark brown, often with paler streaks and slashes. The new bloomy culms that expand quickly through the sheathing are a matte silver blue-grey, creating a two-tone light and dark effect. During the second year, the culms lose their bloom and turn a rich green while the sheaths turn to parchment. The delicate-looking but firmly textured leaves hang gracefully from the high branches, their gloss catching the light and glimmering in the breeze.

Although this forms a large plant, it is rarely a nuisance but I still suggest you give it the space it deserves, as crowding will spoil its individual beauty. If you do plant too closely and have to dig to control it, take note that it has a very tough woody rhizome system and that runs deeper than most. This adds credibility, due to greater tolerance of drought and exposure.

Look out for

Yushania brevipaniculata is a relatively new introduction. It is shorter than *maculata*, but shares a similar stocky habit. New and unusually hairy dark shoots produce pale green culms, while elegant greenery hangs off sparse branching. A mature plant will nearly always be wider than it is high and paler in overall appearance than the other species.

↑ Thinning old or thin culms by cutting and removing at the base

Practicalities for Success

Here are some simple tips for keeping your bamboos in good order in the years ahead, whether newly planted or mature.

Purchasing and Selection

When you buy a bamboo, you are in effect paying for the rhizome inside the pot, rather than the greenery on show above. The root and rhizome are by far the most important parts of the young plant.

Buy a young bamboo whenever possible. Young juvenile plants develop at their own pace and, with a balance of top growth and supporting rhizome structure, often overtake larger specimens in terms of their speed of maturity. If you do insist on buying a large specimen, check with the supplier whether the plant is container grown or containerized. A container-grown plant is one that has been potted on from a young plant throughout its life and has matured equally in rhizome structure and culm formation. A containerized bamboo may have been

↑ Young plants should always appear fresh and green

↓ The healthy root and rhizome of a young bamboo.

lifted from the ground or split from a large stock plant. It may look impressive but the roots and rhizome will have been severed, usually resulting in thin juvenile growth for a year or two as it recovers. I am not saying that a containerized division is not a good plant, just warning you that this reversion back to juvenile growth from mature adult structure is part of the healing process. Some rare bamboos can only be propagated this way.

Ensure the plant is not pale or yellow in colour. If it is, it may be starved and very pot-bound. A fresh green plant is likely to be recently potted and is unlikely to be starved or suffering from a check to its growth. Check for a high percentage of dead or dying culms, which signify that the bamboo may be congested, old, woody and unable to produce new juvenile growth. If possible, also check the roots and rhizomes in the pot. Look for fresh white roots and rhizome, or buds near the edge of the pot or emerging from the surface. If there is an absence of all three, the bamboo may have been very recently potted and is therefore not suitable for transplanting. Also, look closely for visible pests and diseases. Ask whether your supplier uses chemical controls; sometimes plants that have overdosed on chemicals will be weaker in the garden and have no immune system. If the grower uses organic methods, the plants may be stronger and the occasional aphid, although off putting, will usually disappear once the bamboo is planted in your garden.

Buy according to your budget. Three young plants may be a better option than one large specimen, offering greater value in the long term. Large specimens are sometimes slow to establish and often prove to be unstable in the soil after planting. Get as much information as you can when you buy a bamboo (or any plant for that matter). If the person you are buying the plant from cannot tell you a little about it, find someone who can. However, do not expect a guarantee. You are purchasing a living thing and as soon as you take it home it is your responsibility, so make sure you get some advice on how to look after it as well.

Planting, Watering and Nutrition

Planting should always be done with the minimum of ground disturbance. If the soil is over cultivated, it loosens the structure providing less stability for young plants and releases valuable water through evaporation, not to mention bringing weed seeds to the soil surface.

Planting a bamboo can be done almost anytime of year. There is little need to disturb the root mass or any rhizomes as these will find their own way into the soil. The planting hole should be a little larger than the pot and lightly forked. A few handfuls of well-rotted compost can be added to help with water retention, but not directly next to the roots. After planting, lightly tread the soil surface around the new plant, firming it up and keeping it stable in the wind, but take care not to damage any new buds emerging from the root mass. If you plant in the autumn, there is the advantage that the soil will be warm and moist, allowing the plant to partly establish its grip in the soil with little watering to be done. However, a young plant facing its first winter may take a step back in appearance due to the cold and the wind (but not usually to its detriment). Anything planted during spring will certainly need more watering during the first summer than if planted in the autumn, but will be more established for the following winter.

Supplementary watering and feeding have never been provided in my garden. Over the years, the natural organic content of the soil has improved with the decaying leaves of the surrounding broadleaved trees and shrubs and also from the dropping leaves and sheaths of the bamboos. This litter from the bamboo should always be left in situ on the soil surface under the bamboo, as its natural decaying content is one of the best foods for the plant. The organic matter from living plants is the only food my bamboos rely on. I will admit that a new garden created from a building site will often be lacking in both organic and nutrient content and in this situation it would be wise to enrich the soil with rotted manure, garden compost or similar bulky organic material before and after planting for a few years. I am not an advocate of spreading

↑ Be careful not to damage any new buds and shoots when planting

poor soil I would suggest you use one of the new organic supplements on the market. One with a balanced content of NPK (nitrogen, phosphorous and potassium) should suffice and be suited to other plants in your garden. It is possible to speed up the maturity of a bamboo with feeding and watering but do not do this too soon to a juvenile plant. A plant that is just about to reach maturity has a greater demand for sustenance than one that is newly planted.

Mulching with organic matter after planting is to simply cover the soil surface around the new plant with a thin layer about 5 cm (2 in.) deep. Over time this will rot down and provide natural nutrients and fibre, as well as keeping the root-ball either warmer or cooler, depending on the season. Most importantly, the mulch will keep the moisture in the soil longer in between any drying out. Watering of a young plant should only be necessary in the hottest of times or lengthy periods of drought. As the bamboo becomes older and more mature, it will be able to fend for itself with little or no supplement, except perhaps some additional mulching on poor soils. In effect, you should try to duplicate natural surroundings and processes as much as possible.

inorganic fertilizer on to the soil, as this does not happen in nature. Should you need to feed a very

Pruning, Preening and Aftercare

You will be pleased to know that there is very little physical maintenance to be done to either a young or an established bamboo. Here are a few simple tips for keeping the above ground parts in good shape. This information mainly applies to individual plants rather than hedging and screening.

Thin out old culms regularly, especially on many of the taller specimen bamboos with a more open culm structure. On young plants, these will be the original culms from the plant that you purchased, as they will have been superceded by taller, thicker and stronger ones in only a few years. The bamboo naturally diverts its energy into the best and newest growth and naturally stops supplying the older culms with energy, as they have completed their task of helping establish the plant through their photosynthetic processes. Remove the old growth by cutting it away directly above the soil surface.

↑ With time, patience and enthusiasm, it's amazing what you can do with bamboo

↑ A lightly shaped *Chimonobambusa marmorea* (foreground) helps to soften the hard lines of the timber decking

On mature bamboos, each individual culm will live longer, but may need thinning to avoid congestion and for visual effect. Only prune out the oldest, never the new. A bamboo must produce new culms to survive and if these are continually removed the bamboo invariably dies. You will need to invest in some long handled loppers to use on thick culms for their strength and also to access the centre of a large plant.

Some of the growth on young plants may be floppy or arching. This is only because the rhizome has not yet developed its strength in the ground to support the new growth. As the rhizome becomes more substantial, culms will be produced with a more upright habit. There is no harm in taking some top growth from these culms, either by reducing the length of each culm, or by removing some of the branches. This in turn releases some weight and the

culms should spring back to a more vertical position. However, this pruning must only be done when each culm has fully developed its branches or leaves, otherwise it can abort and die-back completely. Occasionally one or two culms may be produced on a mature plant that lean, either due to a lack of support down below or being weakened in very strong winds or heavy snow. These can simply be removed at ground level with no ill effect on the rest of the bamboo.

Unless you are intending to try your hand at formal hedging and screening, I do not recommend shortening of the culms of large growing bamboos as they will always look flat topped and artificial as individual specimens, unless this is the effect you want. It is better to select a bamboo for the maximum height you wish it to grow to, rather than choose something that is potentially too tall. However, it is

↑ These three *Fargesia murielae* have been lightly trimmed to provide a more rounded, formal form as opposed to its usual arching habit

Cutting back almost to the ground of tall bamboos would not seem like common sense unless you were looking to remove them, but many of the lower *Pleioblastus* from Japan do benefit from annual late winter cropping, particularly on established plantings. This purely serves the purpose of generating fresh new and colourful growth for the summer months and stops the plants from becoming congested and lank in habit.

Riot Control and Digging

I am a firm believer that a bamboo should only be planted in a location that is suited to its eventual habit. As an example, an invasive bamboo should not be planted in the smallest of spaces, and as such I do not actively support the use of root and rhizome barriers in the soil. Having made my own mistakes in the past, I do recognize their uses, but I would rather not have made those mistakes in the first place. It is also possible you will inherit a garden full of wrongly planted, aggressive bamboo when you buy a property, and although you might like it, you may need to remove some of it. Hopefully these few tips will help you solve any problems or prevent you from making any similar mistakes in the first place.

possible to shorten branches to create some formality. Many of the more densely branched *Fargesia* species are more suited to branch trimming for formality. The mass of the leaves easily covers the scars.

Culms aborting will likely be a mystery to the beginner. A developing or even mature bamboo can often produce too many culms in one season and some may collapse in a mushy heap within a few days of emergence. Seasonal growing conditions are sometimes the cause, but more likely it is due to growth imbalance and the inability of the rhizome structure below to feed them all. As a result the bamboo puts its energy usually into the best and thickest culms and aborts any that are likely to be weak or inferior. It is more noted on species of *Phyllostachys* and is something you will have to tolerate, but it is not a cause for concern.

- If you do insist on using root and rhizome barriers to keep a bamboo in its place, be aware that in effect you are containing it. As such the plant may require water supplements and more nutrition during times of stress, as when a barrier is installed in the soil, the amount of water and minerals that can be naturally accessed by the bamboo is impeded. I also suggest regular thinning of old culms to keep the plant in balance with its restricted root system. Also consider whether you have to barrier all around the circumference of the bamboo, or can it be done just on one side, for example to prevent it escaping into a neighbouring garden.

↑ Digging a trench around a *Pseudosasa japonica* before putting in a rhizome barrier

↑ The rhizome barrier must protrude above the soil so you can see any escaping rhizomes

- Rhizome barriers are now specially manufactured and many specialist growers do stock them. They are nearly always a shiny black, thick polypropylene material approximately 45 cm (18 in.) wide and sold by the metre. This has to be sunk into the ground at a very slight outward angle from the vertical with a minimum of 5 cm (2 in.) protruding above the ground, so that you can see any invading rhizomes escaping (they rarely go under). Unfortunately the shine of the material remains throughout its life and is not at all

→ A brick edging on a concrete foundation is another alternative for keeping vigorous bamboos in their place

↑ Digging around and undercutting a piece of *Phyllostachys bambusoides* 'Allgold'

pleasing. I prefer using inexpensive concrete slabs of similar width. These can butted closely together or overlapped vertically in the ground and should keep out the most probing of underground growth. As an extra precaution, a stiff silicon sealant can be applied to the joints between the slabs as extra insurance. The advantage of using concrete is that it weathers quickly, becomes stained and mossy and is much less offensive than plastic. Thick timber embedded on a concrete foundation is something I have used as a boundary to pathways, lasting many years and successfully keeping most of my bamboos at bay.

- Should you not wish to use barriers, but still insist on planting something that will potentially creep out of bounds, then you will have to physically control it by removing unwanted rhizomes and culms. It is essential to remove the rhizome rather than just cutting the culms as the rhizome will

have the dormant buds ready to produce more top growth. This method of control is best done in a two year cycle around the bamboo. Remove growth from one side in the first year and then allow it to recover in the next, whilst attacking the other side. Also note that removal within two years of re-growth is easier than leaving it much longer because the rhizomes will be less firmly rooted in the soil, making it easier to remove them.

- If you need to remove a portion of bamboo or the plant as a whole then you will need to dig around the part to be removed. Digging large portions is more successful than just nibbling away at a single culm, as the larger the supporting structure below, the better the chance of the plant's survival. Soil must be attached to the rhizome if possible, in the fashion of a root-ball, best explained as a portion of plant with a firm soil base, rather than rhizome being visible. A trench will have to be dug around the piece to be removed and then the base of the rhizome system can be undercut by at least 45 cm (18 in.). The piece can then be removed and hole filled with extra soil. When transplanting a segment from a mature bamboo, the culm growth that can be expected will not usually match the existing thick culms. The rhizomes have been severed, damaged, mutilated and possibly torn in the removal process and the rhizome buds will also be damaged. Those buds that remain will not have much supporting root structure to nurture them and as a result new culms are likely to be shorter and thinner than those on the parent plant. The division will, more or less, revert back to juvenile in reaction to the severance and use its energy to heal the damage and produce new roots and rhizome for further culm production. The taller more woody bamboos with congested rhizome systems tend to resent disturbance, although some running bamboos thrive on being removed and replanted.

A word of caution – if you do remove a portion

of bamboo and sever the roots, reduce the leaf area of the propagule in proportion. The damaged root system is unlikely to be capable of supplying the top growth with all the required water and nutrients to keep the leaves turgid, thus desiccation can occur. Either prune the culms back in height or remove a quantity in their entirety. Some damage to the mother plant may also be evident where a rhizome that fed culms is left standing.

- To completely eradicate a bamboo you have three alternatives. The first is complete physical removal and by far the most successful and immediate method. The tools for the job range from spades to axes, mattocks and mini-diggers or larger, bearing in mind an established bamboo is a tough beast to remove, and total removal is necessary. Alternatively spray the entire plant with a glyphosate based herbicide that is absorbed by the foliage, spreading downwards into the rhizome and weakening it. After or if the foliage loses its green colouring, cut the entire plant back to the ground. It will more than likely shoot again in subsequent years, but allow it to grow to a point where there is foliage to spray and repeat the above action. The bamboo should become weaker by the year and eventually die out. This is always best done in the warmth of late spring to mid summer. The last and more long term method is very simply to cut the entire plant back, but every time it shoots again, sever it from the rhizomes. If the bamboo is never allowed to take in sunlight through its leaves, it should wear itself out. But beware, the rhizome is an effective storage organ of carbohydrate and has great capacity for shooting many years on. The disadvantage of not removing the entire physical structure of course is that the dead, matted rhizome structure will take many years to rot down, thus making further planting difficult or impossible.

Potential Pests

When you buy a bamboo you can be safe in the knowledge that few pathogens or predators can weaken or damage it, for bamboos in the garden are usually pest and disease free. They are resistant to honey fungus (*Armillaria*) and only occasionally affected by aphids. Attacks from pests usually only occur in the optimum and sometimes forced growing conditions of a commercial nursery. Red spider mite, mealybug, whitefly and aphids are the main problems in this context, but they rarely occur in gardens.

However, in recent years the nuisance of the bamboo mite (*Schizotetranychus celarius*) has spread rapidly from the East to North America and is now seen occasionally in the United Kingdom. The lax import controls within the European Union are largely to blame for the spread of these.

They inhabit the undersides of the leaves and protect themselves with webbing before sucking the

↓ Aphids can secrete a sticky deposit on bamboo leaves, but not to the detriment of the plant

sap from between the veins of a leaf, which results in small pale rectangular patches lacking chlorophyll. The tessellation on many bamboo leaves helps to show up the damage and, as such, makes this pest easy to identify. There are very few bamboo species resistant to this mite and, once you have an infestation, it is difficult to control. Personally, I am not happy about using chemicals on plants but should you choose to use one, a standard miticide may control the pest in its early stages of spread. However, the safest way is to cut the bamboo to the ground and burn all the greenery, rake the surface free of debris and keep a close eye on new emerging growth for further signs of the pest. This may seem drastic but your bamboo will recover eventually. I would stress that the effect on the bamboo is mostly visual and there should be little evidence of poor growth unless the plant is already weak or very young. There are a few types of scale insect that can inhabit the base of

↓ Scale insect at the base of a *Fargesia* culm

culms, mainly seen on *Fargesia* species and *Chusquea*. These are difficult to eradicate chemically and appear to do no harm to the plant, they are easy to wash off with detergent liquid and a fine kitchen scourer.

Rabbits, deer and horses cause physical damage to bamboos by grazing. In general, they favour only the new culms, and there is usually an abundance of other greenery in the summer months for them not to bother with your bamboo. Squirrels like the occasional nibble and giant pandas can be a problem, but fortunately not in our gardens. It is worth noting that mature plants can withstand any attack because of their size. It is always the young plants that are most vunerable, so protect them if you have to.

Very occasionally, physical abnormalities can be seen on bamboos. These are usually quirky in nature and do not have any lasting effect on the plant. Physical damage to a growing point may cause a culm to zigzag (but this zigzag formation does occur naturally as well). Squirrels may gnaw holes in the sides of culms, which sometimes weaken them, but this is rare. One of the more unusual deformities is witches broom, which can occur on the branches of *Phyllostachys*. This distinctive, dense twiggy growth is usually formed because of damage to cells by an insect, virus or fungus, and can sometimes be mistaken for flowering. The deformity is very localised on the plant and has no ill effect on the overall growth. It is more common in China and usually evident on some imported stock.

I have never had need to use an insecticide or fungicide, or similar pesticide. In addition, there has been no need to control animals of any description in my garden, even though it is surrounded by open fields with only a few areas of woodland punctuating the skyline. On the contrary, the bamboos provide a safe haven for many birds roosting at night and, because of their few problems with pests and disease and their ease of cultivation, they are some of the most environmentally friendly plants you could wish for.

Conclusion

"Gardening is all about experimentation and also learning from mistakes, not forgetting that some of the best schemes and plant associations are often created by chance. I would say learn a little first, take heed, then plant as you like. The only thing that matters is that you enjoy the challenge, the fruits of your labour, and take pleasure and pride in the end result."

Glossary

Acute Sharply or narrowly angled.

Aquatic Growing in or living in or near water.

Blade Refers to the true leaf and also the extension at the top of a culm sheath. The true leaf blade is very obvious and an extension of the branch sheath, to which it is linked by a petiole. The true leaf blade is the main site for photosynthesis. The culm sheath blade is less prominent than the true leaf blade, variable in size and occasionally absent. When present, it is capable of photosynthetic activity.

Bigeneric hybrid A hybrid formed when two plants of different genera flower simultaneously in the wild, producing a plant with genetic qualities from both parents.

Bloom Refers to the pale, delicate, powdery surface deposit found particularly on young culms.

Bole, bole-like The shape of a stem or trunk of a tree.

Branch sheath More correctly known as a leaf sheath, it is the scale-like structure on the branches that protects the nodes, buds and emerging tissue of the true leaf. The sheath remains as part of the branch structure with a true leaf attached via a petiole. However, on some species there can be a supplementary sheath at the base of a branch, which is shed and does not produce a true leaf.

Bud A dormant growth point on a rhizome, culm or branch that produces culms, branches and leaves respectively. It appears as a small swelling.

Bulbous Shaped like a bulb or bulging in shape.

Canes Another word for culms (see *culms*) or dried culms.

Clone Plants that originate from a single parent by vegetative propagation and are therefore genetically identical.

Chlorosis (Chlorotic) A nutrient deficiency, usually of iron, which can reduce the green coloration of leaves so they appear yellowish.

Clumping A tight formation of culms.

Clump forming Having a growth habit in which the culms are close together, due to slow rhizome growth.

Continental climate Having wide ranges in temperature, often extreme.

Culm The above-ground stem of a bamboo and other grass-like plants.

Culm leaf The term mostly used in the United States for the culm sheath. This protects and gives support to the emerging culm and, in cases where it is persistent, protects the buds.

Culm sheath The term used for culm leaf throughout this book. See above.

Cultivar A cultivated plant, produced by selective breeding or as a sport or seedling from a garden or nursery rather than the wild.

Deciduous Refers to the shedding of leaves or sheaths during certain seasons, notably winter in the northern hemisphere.

Desiccate Drying out of the leaves through excessive moisture loss.

Die-back Decay from the extremities of the plant downwards towards the root.

Dormant Alive but not in active growth, usually in the winter months.

Ericaceous Referring to an acid (low pH) compost or soil.

Erosion The wearing away of the soil surface by water, wind or rain.

Flora The plants of a particular region.

Foliage The leaves responsible for photosynthetic activity on the ends of the branches.

Foliar Relating to leaves.

Form, forms, f. and forma Refers to a unique characteristic of a plant that has developed in the wild. It usually means a difference in colour or habit from the species.

Friable Easily crumbled soil. Workable.

Genus, genera A group of plants with common

distinct characteristics.

Genetic Refers to the genes of the plant, inherited from its parent or origin.

Geniculation Refers to the lower parts of culms that appears crooked or zigzag in formation on some species. There is no clearly defined reason for this occurrence.

Glaucous A plant surface covered in a fine bluish bloom.

Germinate To sprout, bud or put forth shoots or roots from a seed.

Gregarious flowering Simultaneous flowering of a species or generation of plants, irrespective of their age or location.

Groove See *sulcus*.

Grove A small open grouping of plants or culms.

Habitat The natural home of a group of plants, insects, birds or animals.

Hardy The ability to withstand cold winters.

Hardiness zones Zones of a continent or country that depict the minimum temperature up to which a plant will survive.

Herbaceous perennial A plant whose growth dies down annually but whose roots survive.

Humidity The degree of moisture in the atmosphere.

Husk The dry outer covering of some fruits, seeds or nuts.

Hybrid The offspring of two plants, usually from two different different species.

Internodes The section of a bamboo culm or rhizome between two nodes.

Invasive Tending to spread or encroach on another plants space, usually very quickly.

Juvenile Young or immature.

Lanceolate Long, narrow and tapering at both ends and shaped like a lance head.

Lateral bud Bud at the side of a shoot, root or branch.

Leaf The primary photosynthetic organ of a plant, usually green and flat.

Leaf blade The correct term for the blade attached to the leaf sheath. In other words, the true leaf and main organ for photosynthesis.

Leaf sheath The sheath that encircles a branch and produces a true leaf attached by a petiole.

Leptomorph Refers to a rhizome type usually associated with running bamboos, although there are variations.

Linear Long, narrow and of uniform breadth.

Maritime climate Climate governed by the fact that it is near the sea, so not receiving the extreme temperatures of inland areas.

Montane Of or from a mountainous region.

Mulch, Mulches A mixture spread around the base of a plant to enrich or insulate the soil. Usually bamboo leaves or other organic substances.

Native Originating from a specific area.

Neck Usually refers to the portion joining two growing points on a bamboo and is generally associated with rhizome structure.

Nodes The solid, usually pronounced point on a rhizome, culm or branch where roots, buds, branches, leaves and flowers occur.

Pachymorph Usually associated with clumping bamboos although there are exceptions. This rhizome type turns upwards, always forming a culm that is thinner than the rhizome from which it has been produced.

Palmate With reference to a leaf formation, where three or more leaves emerge from a central point.

Perennial A plant that lives several years, see Herbaceous.

Persistent sheath Refers to a culm sheath that, in general, is not immediately shed and adheres to the culm for a season or more.

Pesticides Substances used for destroying insects or other organisms harmful to cultivated plants.

Petiole The section of leaf sheath that attaches the true leaf to the leaf sheath on a branch.

pH A measure of acidity or alkalinity.

Photosynthesis The process by which the energy of sunlight is used by plants to make carbohydrates from carbon dioxide and water.

Pollinate, pollination Fertilisation of a flower usually resulting in seed production in a bamboo.

Propagation To increase plant stock by division, seed or rhizome cuttings from the parent stock of a bamboo.

Propagule A section of rhizome used for propagation purposes, or a very small division.

Ramify, ramification To cause a plant to branch out and form new subdivisions, offshoots or roots.

Regenerate, regenerative Bring or come into renewed existence again.

Rhizomes The underground stem of the bamboo with a similar structure to the above-ground culm.

Root The part of the plant normally under the ground, attaching it to the soil or compost and through which it takes up water and nutrients to keep the plant alive.

Runners Rhizomes which travel quickly within the soil.

Sheath, sheathing Protective scale-like formation that encircles parts of the culms, branches and rhizomes.

Sheath scar The ring left at the lower part of the node where a sheath was attached.

Shooting season The time of year when most bamboos produce their new shoots. Notably from late spring to early autumn in the northern hemisphere.

Shoots The new growth from a bud that normally grows vertically from ground level or just below.

Slow-release fertiliser Food or nutrient, either in liquid or solid state that is released over a defined, usually long time period.

Species A plant or group of plants belonging to a genus often showing similar but unique characteristics. Distinct forms which occur in the wild.

Specimen An individual plant usually sited on its own.

Sport A mutation on a plant that is different in some way from the appearance of its parent.

Stems The main supporting structure of woody plants.

Striae, striation Thin, linear marks or lines on the surface.

Subspecies, subsp. A group of plants classed as subdivisions of a species, often originating from a geographical location.

Subtropical From the region adjacent to or bordering the tropics.

Sulci, sulcus A groove that runs the length of an internode. This is formed by the development of a prominent bud at the base of the internode that causes the grooving as it develops. Very noticeable in the genus *Phyllostachys*.

Temperate A region or climate characterised by mild to average temperatures.

Tessellation The fine grid-like cross veining of leaves on some species of bamboo. Leaves that are tessellated generally denote cold hardiness, and this structure is only evident on temperate bamboos.

Tillering On bamboo this refers to the production of new culms from the base of existing culms.

Timber bamboo An evergreen, woody bamboo with a permanent, year-round structure.

Transpiration The evaporation of water from the surface of a plant, mostly through the stomata, the minute pores in the surface of a leaf.

Tropical A plant native to the Tropics.

Variegated, variegation Having leaves of more than one colour.

Variety, var. Differing from the species type in some way.

Verdant Green and fresh coloured.

Woody A plant with a structure similar to wood, hard and strong.

Wind pollinated When pollen is transferred from one plant to the next by wind to fertilise the flower.

Where to See and Buy Bamboos

A few specialist nurseries are given below, for further listings contact your country's Bamboo Society.

Internet contacts

European Bamboo Society
  http://www.bamboosocity.org/gbindex.html
American Bamboo Society
  http://www.bamboo.org/abs/

Where to see bamboos

Canada

Butchart Gardens, Victoria, British Columbia.

VanDusen Botanical Gardens, Vancouver, British Columbia.

France

Arboretum de l'École du Breuil, Paris.

Bambous de Planhuisson, Le Buisson de Cadouir National de Brest.

Conservatoire Botanique, Brest, Brittany.

Conservatoire International des Parcs et Jardins, Chaumont-sur-Loire.

La Pagoda, Paris.

Jardin des Plantes, Paris.

Jardin Botanique Exotique du Val Rahmeh, Menton.

Jardins Albert Kahn, Boulogne-Billancourt.

Parc André Citroën, Paris.

Parc Borély, Marseille.

Parc de la Pépinière, Nancy.

Parc de la Tête d'Or, Lyon.

Parc Floral de la Source, Orleans.

Parc Oriental de Maulévrier.

Phoenix Parc Floral de Nice, Nice.

Germany

Bodensee, Mainau Island.

Botanischer Garten und Botanisches Museum, Berlin-Dahlem, Berlin.

Botanischer Garten, München-Nymphenberg.

Grugapark, Essen.

Biozentrum Klein Flottbeck und Botanische Garten, Hamburg.

Palmengarten, Frankfurt.

Botanischer Garten der Friedrich-Willhelms-Universität, Bonn.

Botanischer Garten, Erlangen.

Botanischer Garten der Universität, Karlsruhe.

Botanischer Garten, Oldenburg.

Great Britain

Abbotsbury Subtropical Gardens, Dorchester, Dorset.

Arduaine Gardens, Oban, Argyll.

Bridgemere Garden World, Nantwich, Cheshire.

Carwinion, Falmouth, Cornwall.

Endsleigh House, Milton Abbott, Devon.

Heligan Gardens, St. Austell, Cornwall.

Inverewe Gardens, Gairloch.

Logan Botanics Gardens, Stranraer.

Ness Gardens, Chester, Merseyside.

Portmerion, Porthmadog.

RHS Wisley, Woking, Surrey.

Rosemoor Gardens, Great Torrington, Devon.

Royal Botanic Gardens, Edinburgh.

Royal Botanic Gardens, Kew, Richmond, London.

The Hillier Garden & Arboretum, Romsey, Hampshire.

University Botanic Gardens, Cambridge.

Ireland

Birr Castle, Desmesne, County Cork.

Glasnevin Botanic Garden, Dublin.

Kennedy Arboretum, New Ross, County Wexford.

Mount Usher, Ashford, County Wicklow.

Mucross, Killarney, County Kerry.

Netherlands
Bamboepark Schellinkhout, Schellinkhout.
De Groene Prins, Steenwijkerwold.
Hortus Botanicus, Leiden.
Rotterdam Zoo, Rotterdam.

Switzerland
Botanic Garden Isole di Brissago, Ticino.
Botanic Garden of the University of Basel, Basel.
Botanical Garden of Geneva.
Botanic Garden of the University of Zurich.
Le Centre Horticole de Lulliet, near Geneva.
Chinagarten, Zurich.
Natural History Museum, Winter Garden, Bern.

USA
Arnold Arboretum, Jamaica Plain, Massachusetts.
Avery Island Jungle Garden, Los Angeles, California.
The Bamboo Garden, Foothill College, Northern California.
Brooklyn Botanic Garden, New York.
Hakone Gardens, Saratoga, California.
Live Oak Gardens, New Iberia, Los Angeles, California.
Longwood Gardens, Kenner Square, Pennsylvannia.
Los Angeles State and Country Arboretum, Arcadia, California.
Mercer Arboretum, Philadelphia, Pennsylvania.
North Carolina State Arboretum, Raleigh, North Carolina.
Quail Botanic Gardens, Encinitas, California.
San Diego Zoo and Wild Animal Park, San Diego, California.
Strybing Arboretum and Botanical Gardens, San Francisco, California.
The San Antonio Zoo, San Antonia, Texas.
United States National Arboretum, Washington DC.
University of California Botanic Gardens, California.

Washington Park Arboretum, Seattle, Washington.
Zilker Botanic Garden, Austin, Texas.

Where to buy and see bamboos

Belgium
Bambou du Bois, 113, rue Hubert Bayet, 6180 Courcelles.

France
Bambousaie du Panda, Hameau la Gagnerie, 61 100 La Carneille.
Bambous Lande Diffusion, Route de Orx, 40230 Bennesse-Maremme.
Créa Paysage, Allée de la Roselière-Lannénec, 56270 Ploemeur.
La Bambouseraie de Prafrance, Generargues, 30140, Anduze.
Les Jardins d'Ombre et Lumière, 9 rue Lafayette, 94100 St Maur des Fosses.
Jardin des Collines, 1 rue de Beauvois, 62130 Oeuf en Ternois.
Rezo Plant, "LesVergieres", Montauriol, 47330 Castillonnes.

Germany
Baurnschule, Saarstrasse 3, D-7570, Baden Baden.

Great Britain
Scottish Bamboo Nursery, Middlemuir Farm, Craigievar, Alford, Aberdeenshire AB33 8JS.
Jungle Giants, Ferney Nursies, Onibury, Craven Arms SY7 9BJ.
Just Bamboos, 100 Hayes Lane, Bromley, Kent BR2 9EF.
Pan-Global Plants, The Walled Garden, Frampton Court, Frampton-on-Severn, Gloucestershire GL2 7EX.
PW Plants, Sunnyside, Heath Road, Kenninghall, Norwich, Norfolk NR16 2DS.

The Rodings Plantery, Plot 3, Anchor Lane, Abbess Roding, Essex CM5 0JW.

Ireland

Stam's Bamboo Nursery, Ballinwillin, Lismore, Co. Waterford.

USA

Bamboos 4U, 3625 Gopher, Canyon Road, Vist, CA 92084.

Bamboo Garden, 18900 NW Collins Road, North Plains, Portland, OR 97133.

Bamboo Giant, 5601 Freedom Boulvard, Aptos, CA 95003.

Bamboo Guy Nursery, 24500 Highway, 101 South Beaver, OR 97108.

Bamboo Sourcery, 666 Wagnon Road, Sebastopol, CA 95472.

Blue Heron Farm, 12179 State Route, 530 Rockport, WA 98283.

Burt Associates Bamboo, PO Box 719, 3 Landmark Road, Westford, MA 01886.

David C. Andrews, PO Box 358, Oxon Hill, MD 20750-0358.

Endangered Species, 23280 Stephanie Perris, CA 92570.

Haiku Bamboo Nursery, PO Box 35, Edneyville, NC 28727.

Jade Mountain Bamboo Nursery, 5020-116th Street, Tacoma, WA 98446.

JMBamboo, 4176 Humber road, Dora, AL 35062.

Lewis Bamboo, 121 Creekview Road, Oakman, AL 35579.

Little Acre Farm, 223 Victory Road, Howell, NJ 07731.

Mid Atlantic Bamboos, 1458 Dusty Road, Crewe, VA 23930.

New England Bamboo Co., 5 Granite Street, Rockport, MA 01966.

Redwood Barn Nursery, 1607 Fifth Street, Davis, CA.

Steve Ray's Bamboo Garden, 250 Cedar Cliff Road, Springville, AL 35146.

Shweeash Bamboo, Seaside, OR.

Tradewinds Bamboo Nursery, 28446 Hunters Creek Loop, Gold Beach OR 97444.

Tripple Brook Farm, 37 Middle Road, Southampton, MA 01073.

Canada

Canada's Bamboo World, 8450 Banford Road, Chillwack, British Columbia, V2P 6H3.

Hardiness Zones

Temperatures

$$°C = 5/9 \times (°F - 32)$$
$$°F = (9/5 \times °C) + 32$$

USDA plant hardiness zones

Average Annual Minimum Temperature

Zone	Temperature (°F)	Temperature (°C)
4	−20 to −30	−28.9 to −34.4
5	−10 to −20	−23.4 to −28.8
6	0 to −10	−17.8 to −23.3
7	10 to 0	−12.3 to −17.7
8	20 to 10	−6.7 to −12.2
9	30 to 20	−1.2 to −6.6
10	40 to 30	4.4 to −1.1

To view the U.S. Department of Agriculture Hardiness Zone Map, visit the U.S. National Arboretum site at http://www.usna.usda.gov/Hardzone/ushzmap.html.

Bibliography & Online Resources

Bell, Mike. 2000. *The Gardener's Guide to Growing Temperate Bamboos.* Newton Abbot, Devon: David & Charles. Portland, Oregon: Timber Press.

Crompton, David. 2006. *Ornamental Bamboos.* Portland, Oregon: Timber Press.

Hillier, John and Coombes, Alan. 2002. *The Hillier Manual of Trees & Shrubs.* Newton Abbot, Devon: David & Charles.

Kingsbury, Noël. 2000. *Grasses and Bamboos.* London: Ryland, Peters & Small.

Meredith, Ted Jordan. 2001. *Bamboo for Gardens.* Portland, Oregon: Timber Press.

Recht, Christine and Wetterwald, Max F. 1992. *Bamboos.* London: B.T. Batsford Ltd.

Shilin, Zhu, Naixun, Ma and Maoyi, Fu. 1993. A *Compendium of Chinese Bamboo.* Nanjing: China Forestry Publishing House.

Whittaker, Paul. 2005. *Hardy Bamboos, Taming the Dragon.* Portland, Oregon: Timber Press.

Online resources

(All accessed online in 2009)

ABS American Bamboo Society. Bamboo Information and Pictures. http://www.bambooweb.info/

American Bamboo Society. Growing Bamboos in the Northeast – Promoting the beauty and utility of bamboo.

http://www.americanbamboo.org/GeneralInfoPages/SchneiderIntro.html

Argo farm Bamboo. Frequently Asked Questions. http://www.georgiabamboo.com/Default.aspx?tabid=54

BAM. Bamboo Clothing. http://www.bambooclothing.co.uk/

Bamboo Garden. A bamboo nursery. http://www.bamboogarden.com/

Bamboo Garden at Foothill College. http://www.bamboogarden.org/index.html

Bamboo nursery. Kimmei valkenswaard. http://www.kimmei.com/eng.htm

Bamboo Sourcery. Bamboo. http://www.bamboosourcery.com/

Burt Associates Bamboos. Frequently Asked Questions. http://www.bamboos.com/FAQ.html

Canada Bamboo World. Frequently Asked Questions. http://www.bambooworld.com/faq.htm

Chris Stapleton. Bamboo Identification. http://bamboo-identification.co.uk/html/imposters.html

European Bamboo Society. Links: Information and resources about bamboos from around the world. http://www.bamboosociety.org/links.html

Jade Mountain Bamboo. Growing Bamboo in the Northwest.

http://www.jademountainbamboo.com/html/info/northwest.asp

Jmbamboo Cold Hardy Bamboo Nursery. Bamboo FAQ & More Information. http://www.jmbamboo.com/bamboo_FAQ_information/bamboo_FAQ_information.php

Lewis Bamboo. Bamboo information. http://www.lewisbamboo.com/index.html

Little Acre Farm Bamboo Nursery. Bamboo features. http://www.littleacrefarm.com/bamboo.htm#faq

Mid Atlantic Bamboo. Bamboo information. http://www.midatlanticbamboo.com/index.htm

Multilingual Multiscript Plant Name Database. Sorting Borinda names. http://www.plantnames.unimelb.edu.au/Sorting/Borinda.html

Pan – Global Plants. Bamboo. http://www.panglobalplants.com/plant_nav/plant_code.php?table=bamboo&page=1

Redwood Barn Nursery. Bamboos for the Sacramento Valley. http://redwoodbarn.com/bamboofaqs.html

Sherry and Ralph Boas. Caring for your Bamboo and Frequently Asked Questions. http://www.beautifulbamboo.com/care.php

Shweeash Bamboo. Bamboo care and maintenance. http://www.shweeashbamboo.com/Bamboo%20Care%20and%20Maintenance.htm#bamboo%20photos

Index

Pages in **boldface** include photographs.

Picture Acknowledgements

The author would like to acknowledge the following for granting permission for their photographs to be reproduced in this book.

Diana Whittaker: 31, 34, 48 top, 76 top, 113, 129 top, 134 and 156.

Jane Churly: opposite Introduction, 13, 21 and 115.

Bamboo Garden (especially Noah Bell and Ned Jaquith): 17, 18 left, 20 left, 35, 37 right, 39 right, 40, 44 right, 47, 49, 51 top, 59, 70, 136, 155 left and 157 top right and left.

Marianne Majerus: frontispiece (design: Johan Debecker), 30 left (design: Declan Buckley), 32 (design: Charlotte Rowe), 39 left (design: Lynne Marcus), 45 (design: Catherine Horwood), 46, 48 bottom (photographer, Steven Gunther; design, Mia Lehrer), 51 bottom (Le Jardin de Toru Endo, Jardins, Jardin Aux Tuileries 2008).

All other photographs are by the author.

Many thanks also to the proprietors and directors of these gardens for granting permission for their locations to be photographed either by the author or other photographers.

Mike Ashford, Thurston, Suffolk: 30 right and 138. Bamboo Garden, Portland, Oregon: 17, 18 left, 20 left, 35, 37 right, 39 right, 40, 44 right, 47, 49, 51 top, 59, 70, 136, 155 left, 157 top right and left. La Bambouseraie de Prafrance, Generargues, Anduze: opposite Introduction, 13, 21 and 115. Adrian Bloom, Bressingham, Norfolk: 72, 134 and 156. Peter Boardman, How Hill, Norfolk: 34. Andy Bovington, Lackford, Suffolk: 155 right. John and Marion Clarke, Roydon, Norfolk: 113. Mr Boyd-Jones, Clenchwarton, Norfolk: 33 left, 69, 96 and 140. Stephen Crowe and Fay Ravenhill, North Lopham, Norfolk: 129 bottom. Mike and Sue Daly, North Lopham, Norfolk: 31 and 76 top. Sandra Flint and Stephen Farrow, Banham, Norfolk: 48 top. Carol Maddocks, Attleborough, Norfolk: 129 top. Mr Maurice Mason (deceased), Beachamwell, Norfolk: 83. Plantsman's Preference, South Lopham, Norfolk: 147.